No Evil Star

No Evil Star

Selected Essays,
Interviews, and Prose

ANNE SEXTON

Edited by Steven E. Colburn

Ann Arbor

The University of Michigan Press

Library of Congress Cataloging in Publication Data

Sexton, Anne.
  No evil star.

  (Poets on poetry)
  1. Sexton, Anne—Interviews. 2. Poets, American—
20th century—Interviews. I. Colburn, Steven E.,
1953–   . II. Title. III. Series.
PS3537.E915A6 1985   811'.54   85-8456
ISBN 0-472-06366-9 (pbk.)

*In loving appreciation to my mother and father,
Juanita and Edward Colburn*

Acknowledgments

In appreciation for their invaluable support and assistance at various stages in the completion of this work, grateful acknowledgment is made to the following: Linda Gray Sexton, the poet's daughter; Donald Hall, the series editor; Joan Brandt of The Sterling Lord Agency; Mary Kercz of the Boston Public Library; and Viola C. Ayer and Catherine T. Jones of the Amelia Gayle Gorgas Library, University of Alabama.

Grateful acknowledgment is made to the following publishers and individuals for permission to reprint copyrighted materials:

The Estate of Anne Sexton for the following: "Comment on 'Some Foreign Letters;'" "The Last Believer;" "All God's Children Need Radios;" an interview with Harry Moore; and the uncollected poem "An Obsessive Combination of Ontological Inscape, Trickery and Love."

Houghton Mifflin and the Estate of Anne Sexton for the following poems by Anne Sexton: "Wanting to Die," "Sylvia's Death," "The Addict" from *Live or Die*, copyright © 1966 by Anne Sexton; "Some Foreign Letters," "The Division of Parts," "Unknown Girl in the Maternity Ward" from *To Bedlam and Part Way Back*, copyright © 1960 by Anne Sexton; "All My Pretty Ones," "I Remember," "Young," "Flight," "With Mercy for the Greedy" from *All My Pretty Ones*, copyright © 1962 by Anne Sexton; "The Little Peasant" from *Transformations*, copyright © 1971 by Anne Sexton; "The Fury of Cocks," "The Death Baby" from *The Death Notebooks*, copyright © 1974 by Anne Sexton; "The Rowing Endeth" from *The Awful Rowing*

Editor's Note: This volume collects the best of Anne Sexton's previously published essays, interviews, and prose. Some of the interviews included in part 2 appeared in print considerably after their occasion, a fact I have taken into account in the chronological arrangement of the material.

Contents

An Obsessive Combination of Ontological
Inscape, Trickery and Love

Busy, with an idea for a code, I write
signals hurrying from left to right,
or right to left, by obscure routes,
for my own reasons; taking a word like "writes"
down tiers of tries until its secret rites
make sense; or until, suddenly, RATS
can amazingly and funnily become STAR
and right to left that small star
is mine, for my own liking, to stare
its five lucky pins inside out, to store
forever kindly, as if it were a star
I touched and a miracle I really wrote.

—Anne Sexton
(Uncollected poem published in *Voices:*
A Journal of Poetry 169 [1959]: 34)

I

Essays and Prose

Classroom at Boston University

There are several teachers (and people) named Robert Lowell and I am only going to try to talk about one of them. The Mr. Lowell whom I studied with during the fall of 1958 and the winter of 1959 was a wise man and an accurate teacher. By that I mean that he was usually right about a poem.

The class met at Boston University on Tuesdays from two to four in a dismal room the shape of a shoe box. It was a bleak spot, as if it had been forgotten for years, like the spinning room in Sleeping Beauty's castle. We were not allowed to smoke, but everyone smoked anyhow, using their shoes as ashtrays. Unused to classes of any kind, it seemed slow and uninspired to me. But I had come in through a back door and was no real judge. The summer of 1958 I had made a sort of pilgrimage to meet W. D. Snodgrass at a writer's conference at Antioch. He asked if I had studied with Lowell and insisted that I must—right off.

I had never been to college and knew so little about poetry and other poets that I felt grotesquely out of place in Robert Lowell's graduate seminar. It consisted of some twenty students—seventeen graduates, two other housewives (who were graduate somethings), and a boy who snuck over from M.I.T. I was the only one in that room who hadn't read *Lord Weary's Castle.*

Mr. Lowell was formal in a rather awkward New England

Harvard Advocate 145 (November, 1961). Reprinted with permission.

sense. His voice was soft and slow. It seems to me that people remember the voice of the teacher they loved long after they have forgotten what he said. At least, I have noticed this among poets and their teachers. Mr. Lowell's reverence for John Crowe Ransom's voice was something I wouldn't understand until today as I find myself remembering Lowell's voice and the way *he* would read a poem. At first I felt impatient, packed with ideas and feelings and the desire to interrupt his slow line by line reading of student work. He would read the first line—stop—and then discuss that line at length. I wanted to go through the whole poem quickly and then go back. I couldn't see any merit in dragging through it until you almost hated the damn thing—even your own, especially your own. At that point I wrote Mr. Snodgrass about my impatience and his reply [. . .]* went this way: "Frankly, I used to nod my head at his every statement and he taught me more than a whole gang of scholars could." So I kept my mouth shut. And Snodgrass was right.

Robert Lowell's method of teaching is intuitive and open. After he had read a student poem he always reads another evoked by it. The comparison is often painful. He works with a cold chisel with no more mercy than a dentist. He gets out the decay. But if he is never kind to the poem, he is kind to the poet.

In November I gave him a manuscript to see if he thought "it was a book." He was enthusiastic on the whole, but suggested that I throw out half of it and write another fifteen or so poems that were better. He pointed out the weak ones and I nodded and I took them out. It sounds simple to say that I merely, as he once said, jumped the hurdles that he had put up. But it makes a difference who puts up those hurdles. He defined the goal and acted as though, good race horse that I was, I'd just naturally run the course.

---

*In the interests of maintaining clarity and focus, some brief digressive and redundant passages have been deleted from the interviews and essays as they originally appeared. These are indicated in the text by bracketed ellipses.—Ed.

Since that year and that book I have driven into Marlborough Street twice to see him in his upstairs study. The maid answered the door and I trudged up three long old-fashioned flights of stairs. He sat at his large office-style desk talking in the same slow painstaking manner. One poem, a short lyric, I rewrote seven times until he was satisfied. Robert Lowell's distinction as a poet is that he knows how to control his strength and his distinction as a teacher is that he is never impressed with a display of images or sounds (those things that a poet is born with anyhow).

The last time I saw Mr. Lowell was over a year ago before he left for New York. I miss him as all apprentices miss their first real master. He is a modest man and an incisive critic. He helped me to distrust the easy musical phrase and to look for the frankness of ordinary speech. If you have enough natural energy he can show you how to chain it in. He didn't teach me what to put into a poem, but what to leave out. What he taught me was taste. Perhaps that's the only thing a poet can be taught.

The Bar Fly Ought to Sing

I can add, for Sylvia, only a small sketch and two poems—one poem written for her at the news of her death and the other, written a year later, written directly for both of us and for that place where we met . . . "balanced there, suicides sometimes meet. . . ."

I knew her for a while in Boston. We did grow up in the same suburban town, Wellesley, Massachusetts, but she was about four years behind me and we never met. Even if we had, I wonder if we would have become close friends, back then—she was so bright, so precocious and determined to be special while I was only a pimply boy-crazy thing, flunking most subjects, thinking I was never special. We didn't meet, at any rate, until she was married to Ted Hughes and living in Boston. We met because we were poets. Met, not for protocol, but for truth. She heard, and George Starbuck heard, that I was auditing a class at Boston University given by Robert Lowell. They kind of followed me in, joined me there and so we orbited around the class silently. If we talked at all then we were fools. We knew too much about it to talk. Silence was wiser, when we could command it. We tried, each one in his own manner; sometimes letting our own poems come up, as for a butcher, as for a lover. Both went on. We kept as quiet as possible in view of the father.

"The Bar Fly Ought to Sing" was first published in *Tri Quarterly* 7 (Fall, 1966). Reprinted with permission.

Then, after the class, we would pile into the front seat of my old Ford and I would drive quickly through the traffic to, or near, the Ritz. I would always park illegally in a LOADING ONLY ZONE, telling them gaily, "It's okay, because we are only going to get loaded!" Off we'd go, each on George's arm, into the Ritz and drink three or four or two martinis. George even has a line about this in his first book of poems, *Bone Thoughts*. He wrote, "I *weave with two sweet ladies out of The Ritz.*" Sylvia and I, such sleep mongers, such death mongers, were those two sweet ladies.

In the lounge-bar of the Ritz, not a typical bar at all, but very plush, deep dark red carpeting, red leather chairs around polite little tables and with waiters, white coated and awfully hushed where one knew upon stepping down the five velvet red steps that he was entering *something*, we entered. The waiters knew their job. They waited on the best of Boston, or at least, celebrities. We always hoped they'd make a mistake in our case and think us some strange Hollywood types. There had to be something to explain all our books, our snowboots, our clutter of poems, our oddness, our quick and fiery conversations—and always the weekly threesome hunched around their small but fashionable table.

Often, very often, Sylvia and I would talk at length about our first suicides; at length, in detail and in depth between the free potato chips. Suicide is, after all, the opposite of the poem. Sylvia and I often talked opposites. We talked death with burned-up intensity, both of us drawn to it like moths to an electric light bulb. Sucking on it! She told the story of her first suicide in sweet and loving detail and her description in *The Bell Jar* is just the same story. It is a wonder that we didn't depress George with our egocentricity. Instead, I think, we three were stimulated by it, even George, as if death made each of us a little more real at the moment. Thus we went on, in our fashion, ignoring Lowell and the poems left behind. Poems left behind were technique—lasting but, actually, over. We talked death and this was life for us, lasting in spite of us, or better, because of us, our intent eyes, our fingers clutching the glass, three pairs of eyes fixed on someone's—

each one's gossip. I know that such fascination with death sounds strange (one does not argue that it isn't sick—one knows it *is*—there's no excuse), and that people cannot understand. They keep, every year, each year, asking me "why, why?" So here is the Why-poem, for both of us, those sweet ladies at the Ritz. I do feel somehow that it's the same answer that Sylvia would have given. She's since said it for me in so many poems—so I try to say it for us in one of mine. . . .

Wanting to Die

Since you ask, most days I cannot remember.
I walk in my clothing, unmarked by that voyage.
Then the almost unnameable lust returns.

Even then I have nothing against life.
I know well the grass blades you mention,
the furniture you have placed under the sun.

But suicides have a special language.
Like carpenters they want to know *which tools*.
They never ask *why build*.

Twice I have so simply declared myself,
have possessed the enemy, eaten the enemy,
have taken on his craft, his magic.

In this way, heavy and thoughtful,
warmer than oil or water,
I have rested, drooling at the mouth-hole.

I did not think of my body at needle point.
Even the cornea and the leftover urine were gone.
Suicides have already betrayed the body.

Still-born, they don't always die,
but dazzled, they can't forget a drug so sweet
that even children would look on and smile.

To thrust all that life under your tongue!—
that, all by itself, becomes a passion.
Death's a sad bone; bruised, you'd say,

and yet she waits for me, year after year,
to so delicately undo an old wound,
to empty my breath from its bad prison.

Balanced there, suicides sometimes meet,
raging at the fruit, a pumped-up moon,
leaving the bread they mistook for a kiss,

leaving the page of the book carelessly open,
something unsaid, the phone off the hook
and the love, whatever it was, an infection.

And balanced there we did meet and never asking *why build*—only asking *which tools*. This was our fascination. I neither could nor would give you reasons why either of us wanted *to build*. It is not my place to tell you Sylvia's why nor my desire to tell you mine. But I do say, come picture us exactly at our fragmented meetings, consumed at our passions and at our infections, as we ate five free bowls of potato chips and consumed lots of martinis.

After this we would weave out of the Ritz to spend our last pennies at the Waldorf Cafeteria—a dinner for seventy cents. George was in no hurry. He was separating from his wife. Sylvia's Ted was either able to wait or was busy enough with his own work and I had to stay in the city (I live outside of it) for a seven P.M. appointment with my psychiatrist. A funny three.

I have heard since that Sylvia was determined from childhood to be great, a great writer at the least of it. I tell you, at the time I did not notice this in her. Something told me to bet on her but I never asked it why. I was too determined to bet on myself to actually notice where she was headed in her work. Lowell said, at the time, that he liked her work and that he felt her poems got right to the point. I didn't agree. I felt they really missed the whole point. (These were early poems of hers—poems on the way, on the working toward way.) I told Mr. Lowell that I felt she dodged the point and did so perhaps because of her preoccupation with form. Form was important for Sylvia and each really good poet has one of his own. No matter what he calls it—free verse or what. Still, it belongs to you or it doesn't. Sylvia hadn't then found a form that belonged to her. Those early poems were all in a cage (and not even her own cage at that). I felt she hadn't found a voice of her own, wasn't, in truth, free to be herself. Yet, of course, I knew she was skilled—intense, skilled, perceptive, strange, blonde, lovely, Sylvia.

From England to America we exchanged a few letters. I have them now, of course. She mentions my poems and perhaps I sent her new ones as I wrote—I'm not sure. The time of the LOADING ONLY ZONE was gone as now we sent aerograms back and forth, now and then. George was in Rome. He never wrote. He divorced and remarried over there. Sylvia wrote of one child, keeping bees, another child, my poems—happy, gossip-letters, and then, with silence between us, she died.

After her death, with the printing of her last poems, I read that she gave me credit on a BBC program, credit as an influence upon her work. Certainly she never told me anything about it. But then, maybe she wouldn't have—nothing that ordinary, nothing that direct. She gave me and Robert Lowell (both in a rather casual lump, Sylvia!) credit for our breakthrough into the personal in poetry. I suppose we might have shown her something about daring—daring to tell it true. W. D. Snodgrass showed me in the first place. Perhaps he influenced Robert Lowell too—I can't speak for him. But let's get down to facts. I'm sure Sylvia's influences are hidden, as with most of us, and if one feels compelled to name an influence then let us begin with Theodore Roethke. I remember writing to Sylvia in England after *The Colossus* came out and saying something like: "if you're not careful, Sylvia, you will out-Roethke Roethke," and she replied that I had guessed accurately and that he had been a strong influence on her work. Believe me, no one ever tells one's real influences—and certainly not on the radio or the TV or in interviews, if he can help it. As a matter of fact, I probably guessed wrong and she was lying to me. She ought to. I'd never tell anyone and she was smarter than I am about such hidden things. Poets will not only hide influences. They will bury them! And not that her lines reminded me of Roethke—but the openness to metaphor, the way they both have (and Sylvia even more so in her last work) of jumping straight into their own image and then believing it. No doubt of it—at the end, Sylvia burst from her cage and came riding straight out with the image-ridden-darer, Roethke. But maybe she buried her so-called influence deeper than that, deeper than any one of us would think to look, and if she did I say good luck to her. Her poems do their own work. I don't need to sniff them for distant relatives of some sort. I'm against it. Maybe I did give her a sort of daring, but that's all she should have said. That's all that's similar about our work. Except for death—yes, we have that in common (and there must be enough other poets with that theme to fill an entire library). Never mind last diggings. They don't matter. What matters is her poems. These last poems stun me. They eat time. As for death—

Sylvia's Death
for Sylvia Plath

O Sylvia, Sylvia,
with a dead box of stones and spoons,

with two children, two meteors
wandering loose in the tiny playroom,

with your mouth into the sheet,
into the roofbeam, into the dumb prayer,

(Sylvia, Sylvia,
where did you go
after you wrote me
from Devonshire
about raising potatoes
and keeping bees?)

what did you stand by,
just how did you lie down into?

Thief!—
how did you crawl into,

crawl down alone
into the death I wanted so badly and for so long,

the death we said we both outgrew,
the one we wore on our skinny breasts,

the one we talked of so often each time
we downed three extra dry martinis in Boston,

the death that talked of analysts and cures,
the death that talked like brides with plots,

the death we drank to,
the motives and then the quiet deed?

(In Boston
the dying
ride in cabs,
yes death again,
that ride home
with *our* boy.)

O Sylvia, I remember the sleepy drummer
who beat on our eyes with an old story,

how we wanted to let him come
like a sadist or a New York fairy

to do his job,
a necessity, a window in a wall or a crib,

and since that time he waited
under our heart, our cupboard,

and I see now that we store him up
year after year, old suicides

and I know at the news of your death,
a terrible taste for it, like salt.

(And me,
me too.
And now, Sylvia,
you again
with death again,
that ride home
with *our* boy.)

And I say only
with my arms stretched out into that stone place,

what is your death
but an old belonging,

a mole that fell out
of one of your poems?

(O friend,
while the moon's bad,
and the king's gone,
and the queen's at her wit's end
the bar fly ought to sing!)

O tiny mother,
you too!
O funny duchess!
O blonde thing!

Comment on "Some Foreign Letters"

Some Foreign Letters

I knew you forever and you were always old,
soft white lady of my heart. Surely you would scold
me for sitting up late, reading your letters,
as if these foreign postmarks were meant for me.
You posted them first in London, wearing furs
and a new dress in the winter of eighteen-ninety.
I read how London is dull on Lord Mayor's Day,
where you guided past groups of robbers, the sad holes
of Whitechapel, clutching your pocketbook, on the way
to Jack the Ripper dissecting his famous bones.
This Wednesday in Berlin, you say, you will
go to a bazaar at Bismarck's house. And I
see you as a young girl in a good world still,
writing three generations before mine. I try
to reach into your page and breathe it back . . .
but life is a trick, life is a kitten in a sack.

This is the sack of time your death vacates.
How distant you are on your nickel-plated skates
in the skating park in Berlin, gliding past
me with your Count, while a military band
plays a Strauss waltz. I loved you last,

Poet's Choice, edited by Paul Engle and Joseph Langland (New York: Dial, 1962).

a pleated old lady with a crooked hand.
Once you read *Lohengrin* and every goose
hung high while you practiced castle life
in Hanover. Tonight your letters reduce
history to a guess. The Count had a wife.
You were the old maid aunt who lived with us.
Tonight I read how the winter howled around
the towers of Schloss Schwöbber, how the tedious
language grew in your jaw, how you loved the sound
of the music of the rats tapping on the stone
floors. When you were mine you wore an earphone.

This is Wednesday, May 9th, near Lucerne,
Switzerland, sixty-nine years ago. I learn
your first climb up Mount San Salvatore;
this is the rocky path, the hole in your shoes,
the yankee girl, the iron interior
of her sweet body. You let the Count choose
your next climb. You went together, armed
with alpine stocks, with ham sandwiches
and *seltzer wasser*. You were not alarmed
by the thick woods of briars and bushes,
nor the rugged cliff, nor the first vertigo
up over Lake Lucerne. The Count sweated
with his coat off as you waded through top snow.
He held your hand and kissed you. You rattled
down on the train to catch a steamboat for home;
or other postmarks: Paris, Verona, Rome.

This is Italy. You learn its mother tongue.
I read how you walked on the Palatine among
the ruins of the palaces of the Caesars;
alone in the Roman autumn, alone since July.
When you were mine they wrapped you out of here
with your best hat over your face. I cried
because I was seventeen. I am older now.
I read how your student ticket admitted you
into the private chapel of the Vatican and how
you cheered with the others, as we used to do
on the Fourth of July. One Wednesday in November
you watched a balloon, painted like a silver ball,
float up over the Forum, up over the lost emperors,

to shiver its little modern cage in an occasional
breeze. You worked your New England conscience out
beside artisans, chestnut vendors and the devout.

Tonight I will learn to love you twice;
learn your first days, your mid-Victorian face.
Tonight I will speak up and interrupt
your letters, warning you that wars are coming,
that the Count will die, that you will accept
your America back to live like a prim thing
on the farm in Maine. I tell you, you will come
here, to the suburbs of Boston, to see the blue-nose
world go drunk each night, to see the handsome
children jitterbug, to feel your left ear close
one Friday at Symphony. And I tell you,
you will tip your boot feet out of that hall,
rocking from its sour sound, out onto
the crowded street, letting your spectacles fall
and your hair net tangle as you stop passers-by
to mumble your guilty love while your ears die.

My choice is mostly personal. My special loyalty to "Some
Foreign Letters" stems from its dual outlook toward the past
and the present. It combines them in much the same way that
our lives do—closer to life than to art. It distills a time for me,
a graceful innocent age that I loved but never knew. It is, for
me, like a strange photograph that I come upon each time
with a seizure of despair and astonishment.

"Some Foreign Letters" is a mixture of truth and lies. I
don't feel like confessing which is which. When I wrote it I
attempted to make all of it "true." It remains true *for me* to
this day. But I will say that it was written to my great aunt who
came to live with us when I was about nine and very lonely.
She stayed with us until she had a nervous breakdown. This
was triggered by her sudden deafness. I was seventeen at the
time that she was taken away. She was, during the years she
lived with us, my best friend, my teacher, my confidante and
my comforter. I never thought of her as being young. She was
an extension of myself and was my world. I hadn't considered

that she might have had a world of her own once. Many years later, after her death, I found a bound volume of her letters from Europe. (My family were the type that bound letters in leather.) The letters are gay and intimate and tragic.

The final test of a poem often comes during a public reading. I have almost always read this poem during a "reading" and yet its impact upon me remains strong and utterly personal. I get caught up in it all over again. By the time I get to the last verse my voice begins to break and I, still the public poet, become the private poet who wrote the poem. Because "Some Foreign Letters" still puts a lump in my throat, I know that it is my unconscious favorite. I must always trust such a choice.

The Last Believer

Mary just poked her head around the corner of my writing room. "I've brung the Santa Claus suit down from the attic to warm it up," she told me with her usual sense of timing. Mary works for me and worked for my mother before—"since before you was hatched." After my parents' death two years ago she came here to us part time.

I should have expected her to bring it down, as I've been having Santa Claus problems of my own. The problem is my daughter, Linda, who is eight and a half and ought to be told there isn't a *real* Santa Claus.

"It's the spirit that matters," I tell her. "Now Santa Claus once lived. Historically, he was none other than St. Nicholas, Bishop of Myra, who died in 343 A.D." (I am reading this to her from a pamphlet.) "Our Santa Claus is but an American distortion of the old Dutch name, Sint Niklaas . . ." (I skip a little) "and this goodly man was and is the Patron Saint of Children."

"Now, look here, Linda!" I have stopped reading as she is blocking her ears and puffing out her lower lip. "Honey, I don't mean there isn't *any* Santa Claus. I mean there *really* was such a man and we remember him with presents and. . . ." Now she is crying, the tears rolling thickly and singly through her shut lids.

Vogue, November 15, 1963. Copyright © 1963 by The Condé Nast Publications, Inc.

"Please Mama. I just don't want to discuss it, Mama."

"I just wanted to tell you this nice. . . ."

"You said he died and I don't care what you and Daddy say because that's a lie and he is *too* coming here!"

With that she ran out of the room. She left me sitting here at my desk. I've been trying to tell her for a month but she doesn't want to hear. Her sister is six and isn't the least disturbed, quite capable of hearing me read the pamphlet and of keeping her conviction that jolly old St. Nick will arrive on Christmas Day.

That's the trouble. He will. He always has and I know of no way to stop him. He has been coming since time began for me, since time began for my mother, since time began for my mother's mother, and since time began for my mother's mother's mother. Probably our Santa Claus is older than all the stores in New York City.

I have always lived in the suburbs of Boston—nothing special, in Wellesley as a child and in Newton as a wife and mother. During our childhood, my parents took me and my two sisters to Maine for Christmas. We drove, all jammed together in the trusty Packard, to my grandparents' home in Auburn, Maine.

Auburn was magic. Auburn is where Santa Claus landed. My grandmother's house was built next door to her father's house. The two old homes stood side by side, each with five floors of ample Victorian rooms. Auburn excelled in abundance. There was more snow, more snow than we have ever seen, more colored lights, more relatives, and more talk. The beds were larger and softer.

My bedroom was frosty and the floor boards creaked in the cold, but I was packed down with a comforter and tucked in between flannel sheets. On Christmas night the radiators hissed, chains clacked by on the hill outside, and not a mouse was stirring. We were woken in darkness, dressed hastily in our slippers and robes and were ushered into my grandmother's bedroom to crouch down beside her north window. We were waiting for our first glimpse of Santa's sleigh. We peered out into the semidarkness, our breath fogging the glass, our eyes straining out toward great-grandfather's brick-red house, straining over its weather vanes and peacocks and through the spiny twigs of the oak. We pushed at each other in whispers, feeling the hair rise on our arms in expectation.

"Look! Look! There he is!"

"The sleigh . . . Hello! Hello! The sleigh!"

"Here he comes, here he comes!"

I did see him. I saw the sleigh. I saw Santa sitting up in front and the packages loaded up on the back seat. I heard his terrible laugh ring out as he cracked his long whip across the five A.M. sky. *Ho Prancer!* Indeed, each year I hallucinated the whole show.

Then to the roof. The sleigh had landed. Up in the huge old-fashioned attic, one of my many great-aunts clopped back and forth in grandfather's galoshes, pounding on the attic floor with a wooden stick and shaking a string of sleigh bells. We sat by the window, frozen in our silence and our wonderful mediaeval awe.

Then the large cowbell sounded from the front parlour two floors below. "Merry Christmas!" roared Santa as we ran calling and tumbling down the slippery staircases toward him. Everyone was there, dancing in their night clothes, all the aunts and cousins, my mother in her pink Paisley robe and her pink satin mules, grandfather in his carpet slippers and his L. L. Bean bathrobe. *Merry Christmas!,* shrieked everyone. We kept hugging Santa who was a terribly fat and tall man—a long-haired giant in red with a deep voice from the north. Santa's hug was all-saving and all-beautiful—the embrace of the good woolly lion. No one could have leaned down and hugged me with greater authority. Everyone yelled. We were hysterical. He left, pulling large oranges from his pack and throwing them, like a juggler, high up into the air. "Goodbye Santa. Merry Christmas! Come back! Come back next year!"

And so he did. He came back every year. After the death of my grandparents, Santa chose to come further south. It was much the same, only a different house. It continued like a legacy. However, one year, when I was about ten or eleven, but still sure of his existence, my father was unable to play his customary role (due most likely to an abundance of Christmas cheer the night before). My oldest sister nobly took over. That morning I knew what I had suspected for a year. Her voice just wasn't loud enough. Also she looked like my sister.

However, the year after that there were nearby cousins with small children and my father was back on the job. And then, as the years went by, my oldest sister had children. I remember those years clearly, as I was put in charge of the application of Santa's makeup. My father, warming anew to the rôle now that he was a grandfather, had purchased a new suit at Abercrombie & Fitch. I think it was Abercrombie's, having just researched the facts with Mary who is all-knowing; and having suddenly realized that there is no one left to ask. Mary said, "Abercrumbie's or one of them swell stores." But would Abercrombie's sell Santa Claus suits?

No. Or perhaps they do but he didn't buy it there. I just went upstairs and looked in my husband's closet where the suit is warming up. It says inside the collar "Wolff Fording Co., Theatrical Outfitters, Boston," which shows what an in-expert image both Mary and I have of my father. For of course, theatrical outfitters were more like him, more like the suit.

As the makeup artist I applied rouge to his cheeks, helped strap on the pillows, and put great gobs of clown white on his eyebrows. In those moments, standing in my parents' bathroom, being expert in my teenage field, soothing my father and whispering to him in the five A.M. light, I was closer to him than I had ever been. I applied soot to his shoulders and snow, if we had any. If there was no snow we used frost from the refrigerator, walking together through the half-lit house like thieves. We did it right; the pack, the presents, and never forgot the oranges. Then we collected my mother and my other sister out of their beds and we were off. Daddy walked to his grey Cadillac like an animated cartoon, got in, huffing and grunting over his larger stomach, and turned on the inside light so that we could watch him as he drove. Mother, my sister, and I got into the Ford and drove our car along behind his. We were a miniature caravan of cars driving to my sister's house in another part of Wellesley.

And so it went. After my marriage and my husband's initiation into this early-Christmas-morning madness, my father persuaded him to take over the job, just as, my father told him, he had taken it over from my mother's father.

By now my husband has become a neighborhood institution. At eleven P.M. on Christmas Eve we have to have a dress rehearsal, get the pillows pinned and the straps in place, the boots correct and the beard's earlocks fitted tightly. Then, out he goes; everyone calls to him from their doorway asking him to pose for pictures in front of their fireplace or to peek in on their children and to roar his famous "Merry Christmas" at them. I stand, as always, in the wings.

But I am tired. Perhaps I just miss my father, my grandfather, the winter house in Maine, or all those lost years. Perhaps I am getting old and would like to sleep later on Christmas morning. Or perhaps, in truth, I feel the same old twinge of fear and delight when I look at the big red belly and that long woolly beard. I *have* tried to tell the children, tried to tell them what I know is the truth. I suggest to my husband that we stop all this Santa rigamarole. But he likes being Santa. There isn't any way to stop him. Santa Claus will reappear every year—and each year my childhood will continue to come flaming back, roaring with joy in his large red suit. There is nothing I can do now—except to throw away that pamphlet and go out to buy one dozen navel oranges.

All God's Children Need Radios

Nov. 6, 1971

Thank you for the red roses. They were lovely. Listen, Skeezix, I know you didn't give them to me, but I like to pretend you did because, as you know, when you give me something my heart faints on the pillow. Well, someone gave them to me, some official, some bureaucrat, it seems, gave me these one dozen. They lived a day and a half, little cups of blood, twelve baby fists. Dead today in their vase. They are a cold people. I don't throw them out, I keep them as a memento of my first abortion. They smell like a Woolworth's, half between the candy counter and the 99-cent perfume. Sorry they're dead, but thanks anyhow. I wanted daisies. I never said, but I wanted daisies. I would have taken care of daisies, giving them an aspirin every hour and cutting their stems properly, but with roses I'm reckless. When they arrive in their long white box, they're already in the death house.

Trout

Same day

The trout (brook) are sitting in the green plastic garbage pail full of pond water. They are Dr. M's trout, from his stocked

---

Originally appeared as "A Small Journal" in *Ms.* magazine, November, 1973. Reprinted with permission.

pond. They are doomed. If I don't hurry and get this down, we will have broken their necks (backs?) and fried them in the black skillet and eaten them with our silver forks and forgotten all about them. Doomed. There they are nose to nose, wiggling in their cell, awaiting their execution. I like trout, as you know, but that pail is too close and I keep peering into it. We want them fresh, don't we? So be it. From the pond to the pail to the pan to the belly to the toilet. We'll have broccoli with hollandaise. Does broccoli have a soul? The trout soil themselves. Fishing is not humane or good for business.

Some Things Around My Desk

Same day

If you put your ear close to a book, you can hear it talking. A tin voice, very small, somewhat like a puppet, asexual. Yet all at once? Over my head JOHN BROWN'S BODY is dictating to EROTIC POETRY. And so forth. The postage scale sits like a pregnant secretary. I bought it thirteen years ago. It thinks a letter goes for 4 cents. So much for inflation, so much for secretaries. The calendar, upper left, is covered with psychiatrists. They are having a meeting on my November. Then there are some anonymous quotations Scotch-taped up. *Poets and pigs are not appreciated until they are dead.* And: *The more I write, the more the silence seems to be eating away at me.* And here is Pushkin, not quite anonymous: *And reading my own life with loathing, I tremble and curse.* And: *Unhappiness is more beautiful when seen through a window than from within.* And so forth. Sweeney's telegram is also up there. *You are lucky,* he cables. Are you jealous? No, you are reading the Town Report, frequently you read something aloud and it almost mixes up my meditations. Now you're looking at the trout. Doomed. My mother's picture is on the right up above the desk. When that picture was taken, she too was doomed. You read aloud: *Forty-five dog bites in town.* Not us. Our dog bites frogs only. *Five runaways and five stubborn children.* Not us. Children stubborn but not reported. The phone, at my back and a little to the right, sits like a general (German) (SS). It holds the voices that

I love as well as strangers, a platoon of beggars asking me to dress their wounds. The trout are getting peppier. My mother seems to be looking at them. Speaking of the phone, yesterday Sweeney called from Australia to wish me a happy birthday. (Wrong day. I'm November ninth.) I put my books on the line and they said, "Move along, Buster." And why not? All things made lovely are doomed. *Two cases of chancres,* you read.

Eat and Sleep

Nov. 7, 1971

Today I threw the roses out, and before they died the trout spawned. We ate them anyhow with a wine bottled in the year I was born (1928). The meal was good, but I preferred them alive. So much for gourmet cooking. Today the funeral meats, out to Webster (you call it Ethan Frome country) for a wake. *Eat* and *Sleep* signs. World War II steel helmets for sale. There was a church with a statue of a mother in front of it. You know, one of those mothers. The corpse clutched his rosary and his cheek bumped the Stars and Stripes. A big man, he was somebody's father. But what in hell was that red book? Was it a prayer book or a passport at his side? Passports are blue, but mine has a red case. I like to think it's his passport, a union card for the final crossing. On the drive back, fields of burst milkweed and the sun setting against hog-black winter clouds. It was a nice drive. We saw many *Eat* and *Sleep* signs. Last night the eater, today the sleeper.

Mother's Radio

Nov. 8, 1971

FM please and as few ads as possible. One beside my place in the kitchen where I sit in a doze in the winter sun, letting the warmth and music ooze through me. One at my bed too. I call them both: *Mother's Radio.* As she lay dying her radio played, it played her to sleep, it played for my vigil, and then one day the nurse said, "Here, take it." Mother was in her coma, never, never to say again, "This is the baby," referring to me at any age. Coma that kept her under water, her gills pumping, her brain numb. I took the radio, my vigil keeper, and played it for my waking, sleeping ever since. In memoriam. It goes everywhere with me like a dog on a leash. Took it to a love affair, peopling the bare rented room. We drank wine and ate cheese and let it play. No ads please. FM only. When I go to a mental hospital I have it in my hand. I sign myself in (voluntary commitment papers) accompanied by cigarettes and mother's radio. The hospital is suspicious of these things because they do not understand that I bring my mother with me, her cigarettes, her radio. Thus I am not alone. Generally speaking mental hospitals are lonely places, they are full of TV's and medications. I have found a station that plays the hit tunes of the nineteen-forties, and I dance in the kitchen, snapping my fingers. My daughters laugh and talk about bobby socks. I will die with this radio playing—last sounds. My children will hold up my books and I will say good-bye to them. I wish I hadn't taken it when she was in a coma. Maybe she regained consciousness for a moment and looked for that familiar black box. Maybe the nurse left the room for a moment and there was my mama looking for her familiars. Maybe she could hear the nurse tell me to take it. I didn't know what I was doing. I'd never seen anyone die before. I wish I hadn't. Oh Mama, forgive. I keep it going; it never stops. They will say of me, "Describe her, please." And you will answer, "She played the radio a lot." When I go out it plays— to keep the puppy company. It is fetal. It is her heartbeat— oh my black sound box, I love you! Mama, mama, play on!

Little Girl, Big Doll

Nov. 10, 1971

Out my window, a little girl walking down the street in a fat and fuzzy coat, carrying a big doll. Hugging it. The doll is almost as large as a basset hound. The doll with a pink dress and bare feet. Yesterday was my birthday and I excised it with bourbon. No one gave me a big doll. Yesterday I received one yellow wastebasket, two umbrellas, one navy pocketbook, two

Pyrex dishes, one pill pot, one ornate and grotesque brown hamper. No doll. The man in the casket is gone. The birthday is gone, but the little girl skipped by under the wrinkled oak leaves and held fast to a replica of herself. I had a Dye-dee doll myself, a Cinderella doll with a crown made of diamonds and a Raggedy Ann with orange hair and once on my sixth birthday a big doll, almost my size. Her eyes were brown and her name was Amanda and she did not welcome death. Death forgot her. (For the time being.)

Daddy Sugar

Nov. 15, 1971

O. called the night before my birthday, sticking his senile red tongue into the phone. Yet sentimental too, saying how it was forty-three years ago, that night when he paced the floor of my birth. I never heard of my father pacing the floor—a third child, he was bored. Isn't pacing limited to fathers? That's the point, isn't it! Maybe O. is my biological father, my daddy sugar and sperm. It ruined my birthday, to be claimed at forty-three by O. Just last Christmas, around the twentieth of December, he arrived out here with a secret package—my photo at sixteen (I never gave it to him. Mother must have given it to him!) and a lock of my baby hair. Why would Mother give a lock of baby hair to bachelor-family-friend-O.? He said, "I don't want to die with the evidence!" And then he drove off. Later, on the phone we promise to meet for lunch and have a confession hour. But I shy away. I am like Jocasta who begs Oedipus not to look further. I am a dog refusing poisoned meat. It would be poison he pumped into my mother. She who made me. But who with? I'm afraid of that lunch—I would throw up the vichyssoise if he said: "Happy birthday, Anne, I am your father."

Brown Leaves

Nov. 16, 1971

Out my window: some wonderful blue sky. Also I see brown leaves, wrinkled things, the color of my father's suitcases. All

27

winter long these leaves will hang there—the light glinting off them as off a cow. At this moment I am drinking. At this moment I am very broke. I called my agent but she wasn't there, only the brown leaves are there. They whisper, "We are wiser than money; don't spend us." . . . And the two trees, my two telephone poles, simply wait. Wait for what? More words, dummy! Joy, who is as straight as a tree, is bent today like a spatula. I will take her to the orthopedic man. Speaking of suitcases, I think of my childhood and MUTNICK FOREVER. Christmases, every single year, my father tearing off the red wrapping and finding a Mark Cross two-suiter, calf, calf the color of the oak leaves—and thinking of the wool supplier, Mr. Mutnick, who gave him this yearly goodie— he'd cry, "MUTNICK FOREVER." That sound, those two words meant suitcases, light tan, the color of dog shit but as soft as a baby's cheek and smelling of leather and horse.

Breathing Toys

Nov. 18, 1971
The gentle wind, the kind gentle wind, goes in and out of me. But not too well. Walking a block—just say from Beacon to Commonwealth—or over at B.U., I lean against the building for wind, gasping like a snorkel, the crazy seizure of the heart, the error of the lungs. Dr. M. wants me to go into his hospital for tests, come January. He's a strange one, aside from his stocked trout pool he keeps saying, "I want to save a life!" The life being mine. Last time we met he said, "You'll be an old hag in three years!" What does he mean? A yellow woman with wax teeth and charcoal ringlets at her neck? Or does he only mean the breathing—the air is hiding, the air will not do! An old hag, her breasts shrunken to the size of pearls? My lungs, those little animals, contracting, drowning in their shell. . . . Joy is still down. Meals float up to her. (I am the cork.) She lies on her mattress with a board under it and asks, "Why me?" Her little toes wriggling on the roof, her head lolling over the TV, her back washing like sand at low tide. As I've said elsewhere: the body is meat. Joy, will you and I

outlive our doctors or will we oblige, sinking downward as they turn off the flame? As for me, it's the cigarettes, of course. I can't give them up any more than I can give up Mother's radio. I didn't always smoke. Once I was a baby. Back then only Mother smoked. It hurts, Mama, it hurts to suck on the moon through the bars. Mama, smoke curls out of your lips and you sing me a lullaby. Mama, mama, you hurt too much, you make no sense, you give me a breathing toy from World War II and now you take it away. Which war is this, Mama, with the guns smoking and you making no sense with cigarettes?

Dog

Nov. 19, 1971

"O Lord," they said last night on TV, "the sea is so mighty and my dog is so small." I *heard* dog. You say, they said *boat* not *dog* and that further *dog* would have no meaning. But it does mean. The sea is mother-death and she is a mighty female, the one who wins, the one who sucks us all up. *Dog* stands for me and the new puppy, Daisy. I wouldn't have kept her if we hadn't named her Daisy. (You brought me daisies yesterday, not roses, daisies. A proper flower. It outlives any other in its little vessel of water. You must have given them to me! If you didn't give them to me, who did?) Me and my dog, my Dalmatian dog, against the world. "My dog is so small" means that even the two of us will be stamped under. Further, dog is what's in the sky on winter mornings. Sun-dogs springing back and forth across the sky. But we dogs are small and the sun will burn us down and the sea has our number. Oh Lord, the sea is so mighty and my dog is so small, my dog whom I sail with into the west. The sea is mother, larger than Asia, both lowering their large breasts onto the coastline. Thus we ride on her praying for good moods and a smile in the heavens. She is mighty, oh Lord, but I with my little puppy, Daisy, remain a child.

Too complicated, eh?

Just a thought in passing, just something about a lady and her dog, setting forth as they do, on a new life.

Thanksgiving in Fat City

Nov. 25, 1971

The turkey glows. It has been electrified. The legs huddle, they are bears. The breasts sit, dying out, and the gizzard waits like a wart. Everyone eats, hook and sinker, they eat. They eat like a lady and a bear. They eat like a drowning dog. The house sits like the turkey. The chimney gasps for breath and the large, large rock on the front lawn is waiting for us to move into it. It is a large mouth. Autograph seekers attend it. They mail it letters, postage due. They raise their skirts and tease it. . . . It is a camera, it records the mailman, it records the gasman, it records the needy students, it records the lovers, serious as grandmothers, it records the sun and the poisonous gases, it records the eaters, the turkey, the drowned dog, the autograph seekers, the whole Hollywood trip. Meanwhile I sit inside like a crab at my desk, typing pebbles into a boat.

A Life of Things

Dec. 2, 1971

They live a life of things, Williams said. This house is stuffed like a pepper with things: the painted eyes of my mother crack in the attic, the blue dress I went mad in is carved on the cameo. Time is passing, say the shoes. Afrika boots saying their numbers, wedding slippers raining on the attic floor. The radiator swallows, digesting its gallstones. The sink opens its mouth like a watermelon. Hadn't I better move out, dragging behind me the bare essentials: a few pills, a few books, and a blanket for sleeping? When I die, who will put it all away? Who will index the letters, the books, the names, the expendable jewels of a life? Things sweat in my palm as I put them each carefully into my mouth and swallow. Each one a baby. Let me give the jar of honey, the pickles, the salt box to my birthday. Let me give the desk and its elephant to the postman. Let me give the giant bed to the willow so that she may haunt it. Let me give the hat, the Italian-made Safari hat, to my dog so that she may chew off her puppyhood. Finally let me give the house itself to Mary-who-comes. Mary-who-comes has scoured the floors of my childhood and the floors of my motherhood. She of the dogs, the army of dogs, old English Sheep dogs (best of show), fifteen altogether, their eyes shy and hidden by hair, their bodies curled up wool. Mary-who-comes may have my house: the Lenox for her dogs to lap, the kitchen for breeding, the writing room for combing and currying. Mary will have a temple, a dog temple, and I will have divorced my things and gone on to other strangers.

Found Topaz

Dec. 10, 1971
The sherry in its glass on the kitchen table, reflecting the winter sun, is a liquid topaz. It makes a tinkerbelle light on the wall. Sea light, terror light, laugh light. . . . There is less and less sherry, a cocktail sherry, very light, very good. It keeps me company. I am swallowing jewels, light by light. To celebrate this moment (it is like being in love) I am having a cigarette. Fire in the mouth. Topaz in the stomach.

Oatmeal Spoons

Same day
I am still in the kitchen, feeling the heat of the sun through the storm window, letting Mother's radio play its little tunes. Dr. Brundig is away, a week now, and I'm okay, I'm sanforized, above ground, full of anonymous language, a sherry destiny, grinning, proud as a kid with a new drawing. I'm flying invisible balloons from my mailbox and I'd like to give a party and ask my past in. And you—I tell you how great I feel and you look doubtful, a sour look as if you were sucking the ocean out of an olive. You figure, she's spent fifteen years attending classes with Dr. Brundig and her cohorts, majoring in dependence. Dr. M. (trout man, lung man) asked me, "What is your major problem? Surely you know after fifteen years?"
"Dunno."

"Well," he said, "Did you fall in love with your oatmeal spoon?"

"There was no oatmeal spoon."

He caught on.

Angels Wooly Angels

Jan. 1, 1972, 12:30 A.M.

I feel mild. Mild and kind. I am quite alone this New Year's Eve for you are sick: having fallen in love with the toilet, you went on an opium voyage and fell asleep before the New Year. I heard it all down here in the kitchen on Mother's radio—Times Square and all that folly. I am drinking champagne and burping up my childhood: champagne on Christmas Day with my father planting corks in the ceiling and the aunts and uncles clapping, Mother's diamonds making mirrors of the candlelight, the grandmothers laughing like stuffed pillows and the love that was endless for one day. We held hands and danced around the tree singing our own tribal song. (Written in the eighteen hundreds by a great, great uncle.) We were happy, happy, happy. Daddy crying his MUTNICK FOREVER and the big doll, Amanda, that I got. . . . All dead now. The doll lies in her grave, a horse fetus, her china blue eyes as white as eggs. Now I am the wife. I am the mother. You are the uncles, the grandmothers. We are the Christmas. Something gets passed on—a certain zest for the tribe, along with the champagne, the cold lobster hors d'oeuvres, the song. Mother, I love you and it doesn't matter about O. It doesn't matter who my father was; it matters who I *remember* he was. There was a queen. There was a king. There were three princesses. That's the whole story. I swear it on my wallet. I swear it on my radio. See, Mother, there are angels flying over my house tonight. They wear American Legion hats but the rest of them is wool, wool, that white fluffy stuff Daddy used to manufacture into goods, wool, fat fleecy wool. They zing over the telephone wires, their furry wings going *Hush, hush.* Like a mother comforting a child.

The Freak Show

One way poets make a living, make it by their own wits, [. . .] is by giving readings. On January 4, 1973, I stopped giving readings, and believe me, I needed the money. Furthermore, I asked such preposterous sums that I gave fewer readings than most poets do.

What's in it for the poet? Money, applause, adulation, someone to hear how the poems sound coming out of the poet's mouth, an audience. Don't kid yourself. You write for an audience (I think of myself as writing for one person, that one perfect reader who understands and loves). If the audiences were this one person multiplied by a hundred or a thousand, everything would be okeydokey.

From my limited experience, it does not go that way. You are the freak. You are the actor, the clown, the oddball. Some people come to see what you look like, what you have on, what your voice sounds like. Some people secretly hope your voice will tremble (that gives an extra kick). Some people hope you will do something audacious, in other words (and I admit to my greatest fears) that you vomit on the stage or go blind, hysterically blind or actually blind.

Once at a college in New Hampshire, I cried after I read a poem. I had never read this poem before an audience, and I had no idea it would move me so. I was embarrassed to cry. I

"The Freak Show" appeared originally in the May/June, 1973, issue of the *American Poetry Review*. Reprinted with permission.

had to go offstage and get my pocketbook, which had a Kleenex in it, so that I might blow my nose. The audience cheered. Maybe they didn't cheer because it was more of a show to see me cry. Maybe they only meant, "Anne, we're with you."

However, it was reported to me that my lecture bureau (one of their agents happened to be in my audience that night when I cried) speaks proudly of my presentation to their clients thusly: "It's a great show! Really a pow! She cries every time right on stage!"

Watch out for those lecture bureaus. They may get you bookings, they may get you more money, but they exploit your soul in ways such as these.

At the last reading I gave, at a luncheon before the reading with many professors (at universities all over the United States you can meet some of the kindest, most soulful, dearest people—once in a while some of the most cruel) who ate and drank with me and did their best to hold me up, for I drink like a drunkard before a reading because I am so scared.

I was so sure I was to die flying out there to the Midwest, that the plane would crash, fall like the *Hindenburg* from the sky, but it was a different death that came about—the death of Anne as a performer. I was met (alive) by a very sweet and understanding English professor, who also happened to like poetry. We had a beer at the airport, and I vented my feelings about readings and how poets shouldn't give them, and he listened with compassion, but without comprehension.

Then the drive into the city and the luncheon at the student bistro, a barnlike place, our table on top of a hot but fake fireplace, four men and one token woman professor, Janet Beeler. She was seated as far from me as possible, so that we kind of had to yell out our sisterhood, our commonwealth of similar sensibilities. I could feel her compassion as I guzzled down the double vodkas, once even with vomit rising in my throat and me swallowing it—not vomit because I was drunk, but because I was drinking too fast and I was scared.

At that point all immediately said, "Let's go out and get you some air." I replied very softly, "I don't need air. If you'd only just be quiet for a moment, I'll get hold of myself." The men immediately started talking as fast as possible (not comprehending my request), and Janet Beeler hushed them and reminded them of my request.

Later the man who had arranged the reading, a vibrant, attractive, understanding type, although one felt he had never read any poetry, walked out to the chef and got me a western sandwich, because previously I had only picked at a badly burned hamburger and had said wistfully, "The luckiest thing for me to eat before a reading is a western sandwich." Three good omens: I was alive, there was an understanding sister, and a western sandwich. I would indeed be able to give the reading.

One professor who was, as I recall, in business law, told me he was forcing fifty of his business students to come to my reading, although they knew nothing about poetry. I said, "Thanks a lot," meaning thanks for sticking fifty bodies in the audience who do not like poetry and will see *nothing* but the freak.

Poetry is for us poets the handwriting on the tablet of the soul. It is the most private, deepest, most precious part of us. Yet somehow in this poetry biz, as one of my students calls it, we are asked to make a show of it. [. . .]

I don't feel this way about New York audiences. I'll tell you why. For some reason unexplainable to me, the audiences I have had at the Y or the Guggenheim seem to have read my poetry from the very beginning and want to hear the new stuff or the old stuff just because they want to know what it sounds like when I say it. The last time I read at the Y and I had a temperature of 104 and bad bronchitis, a man yelled up from the audience as I was speaking (forgive me; I can never remember quotes or dialogue correctly—I can only approximate), "Whatever you do, Annie, baby, we're with you."

Once at the Hatch Shell in Boston, after I was introduced by the huckster (wine company PR man) who was paying for the reading, someone screamed out, "Long live Anne Sexton." Those two voices will remain in my head forever. I do know there are many who do not yell, all over the country, but feel that way. I can only say to them, "God bless you."

I remember being a fledgling poet and going to hear the famous poets read. I wanted to hear what they had to say, but there was a sneaky, unconscious, underground part of me that wanted the poet to be a little weird. Why? I think all of us poets feel so alien inside, so alien from the world, that we want the big names to act a little alien, a little crazy, just to confirm what is in the deepest soul of the young poet.

I have been told often what a thrill it was to see if poor but wonderful Dylan Thomas would last through the reading on all that booze. I have also been told of W. H. Auden coming on stage absentmindedly in his carpet slippers, and how delighted the poets and others were to observe such a unique characteristic in one of the world's great poets, etc., etc.

I find that a poetry reading takes a month from my writing—the trauma. I spoke to a dear friend, a very famous poet—you would all know him—and he said after a certain reading, he came home and his nose bled for three days. He, too, was going to give up readings. He will need the money from the readings. It is a way of getting by. But I ask all you poets what in hell are we doing to ourselves—why are we making ourselves into freaks when we are really some sort of priest or prophet or hermit. I ask you audiences to look deeply into yourselves before you go to the poetry reading and say, "What is it I want of this person, this human being, who is going to reveal his deepest thoughts?" If any of you have any answers, I would be glad to listen.

That was supposed to be the end of this column, but yesterday, February 24, the answer came. It came to my mailbox at Boston University (a place I seldom investigate—thus the delay). Here is the letter from one Janet Beeler:

Thursday night, Jan. 4th

Dear Anne,

I feel like I need to close the experience of this day by writing a note to you with a kind of oblique blessing of some sort—Oh, I hope you're home safely by now, snug and warm and protected. I wish you well, my friend.

I really don't know what to think about that surrealistic lunch—the overheated room, the strange food, the awkwardness of even the chairs.

Those men treated you in such a strange way—as though you thought of yourself as a kind of expensive freak. No, that's not it—they wanted to please, but didn't know how, so were patronizing, brusque, adolescent. And you of all people seem so worth protecting, and were so unprotected. I was very moved by you today—by who you are, or seemed to be. You seemed defenseless, for such a tough cookie. And I felt for your anxiety, and the attempts you make to get some distance from it, and what is happening, and to handle the various frustrations and pains and challenges.

Listen, the reading was fine. Oh, I was prejudiced, but I mean that I took care to ask some of the trapped Business Law kids what they thought. It seems important to tell you that one boy said, "It was mysterious." I take that as an affirmative compliment—good for him, he felt the mystery. The people I know that read you anyway were very positive—felt satisfied, even fortified. Maybe you don't care about that kind of news, but I did—I was fascinated—what would they make of those words! The contrasts of the profound meanings and the simple vocabulary struck one girl—well, good for her, too.

The only thing I'm feeling now is hungry—I wanted some time to talk. Isn't it strange, to have lived with you all these years—the poems among the last at night (in the company of Pound, Neruda, Rilke, my favorites)—to have lived through those parts of you, for your thoughts to have been part of my life, an intimate part. If you wrote different poetry—if you wrote farther from your marrow, it wouldn't be so. But there it is: my friend, the one who knows. And there you are. And I want to talk to you. Selfishly. I want to know the news from the fatherland, the news from the front. And the kids, how are they now? And you, what are the good things now? As though you owed that in some way because you've shared the bad news. And of course you don't have to share anything at all. It's just that . . . well, we've lived together. I'm sorry, Anne. I feel I'm grabbing, but it's a powerful feeling in me. It's okay.

Well, look, I want to do something. You don't have to do anything about it, for Christ's sake, but I want to share something of myself with you. I've been writing too, for several years—never had much audience, or exposed myself, but these three poems were accepted by *Antaeus*. Anyway, I want to share them with you. You don't have to do anything, don't even read them if you're working. I just want something mutual, because your work is a precious part of my life. And I liked you a lot today. A lot.

Part of the blessing is that you have a good new year—new life, sweet new beginnings. If you have to come to Cleveland again, let me see you?

Love,

Janet Beeler

Who knows? Some day I may go forth on some jet to some college and look for that one person again and read my goddamned heart out.

II

Interviews

With Harry Moore

[In this edited transcript of a telephone conference call, Harry Moore serves as moderator for the interview, introducing and commenting upon questions by the students of Stephens College, Langston University, Morehouse College, Jackson State College, Drury College, and Tougaloo Southern Christian College.—ED.]

Anne Sexton, born in Newton, Massachusetts, in 1928, now lives in Newton Lower Falls, not far from her birthplace. She attended Boston University without taking a degree; while there studied poetry with Robert Lowell. Since 1957 her verse has appeared in journals such as the Antioch Review, *the* Hudson Review, *and the* Partisan Review *as well as in such mass-circulation magazines as* Harper's *and the* New Yorker. *In 1959 Mrs. Sexton was granted the Robert Frost Fellowship to study at the Bread Loaf School, and in the following year she brought out her first book of poems,* To Bedlam and Part Way Back, *followed in 1962 by* All My Pretty Ones, *and in 1966 by* Live or Die, *which won the Pulitzer Prize. In 1962 she became the first traveling fellow in poetry of the American Academy of Arts and Letters. Mrs. Sexton has taught a class in the writing of verse at the Radcliffe Institute for Independent Study and has been elected a Fellow of the Royal Society of Literature of the United Kingdom. With Maxine Kumin she has written* Eggs of Things, *a book for*

Talks with Authors, edited by Charles F. Madden (Carbondale: Southern Illinois University Press, 1968).

elementary school children. In her poetry for mature readers, Mrs. Sexton is unusually candid, and a good deal of her verse is a direct rendering—in dexterous technique—of raw experience, combined with the poet's reflections. The circumstances of her life have not always been happy, and yet she is often a poet of the joy of existence as found in natural phenomena. Her New England background is one of the salient features of her writings and its geography—Boston and the Maine coast and Cape Cod—continually manifests itself. But this poet seems concerned most of all with family life, and some of her most skillful poems are family portraits which are examined with a tinge of nostalgia, a sense of guilt, and, most predominant, a harrowing ability to see the skull beneath the skin. In the conversation which follows, Mrs. Sexton undertakes a rare approach by giving over her introductory time to an intimately technical discussion of the creation of one of those poems. Her works selected for study on the present occasion are: "All My Pretty Ones," "Flight," "The Division of Parts," "I Remember," and "Young."

Moore: We've had a great deal about the Midwest and the South; now we're going to New England. Mrs. Sexton is, as you know, one of the most highly thought of younger poets. She's going to take about ten minutes to present a very interesting project here before we have our questions. Mrs. Sexton.

Sexton: Well, I thought instead of making general comments I'd try to make a few specific comments on how one poem started, got off the ground. Every poet has a lot of unwritten poems in him, and every poem that does exist is one where he got lucky, where he was stubborn enough to drag a poem into existence. For me each poem has its own sound or its own voice or its own form, whatever you want to call it. Until I find it I'm crawling in the dark or through mud. The poem I thought I would look at in detail is "All My Pretty Ones," which is among the copies of my work that everyone has.

I have here, on my desk, six pages of beginning worksheets

of "All My Pretty Ones." I thought I would read you parts from each page so you might see, line by line, how very badly it began, and how it almost never got written. I'm not sure of the time lapse as I read it. I have these five or six pages and perhaps they cover a week of attempts. I don't remember.

The title was given to me by a friend who stole it from Shakespeare in the first place. She wrote me a condolence note after my father's death and I received it, I think, as I was working on the poem. She said in her letter, "Oh no, Anne, your mother in March and your father in June. All your pretty ones at once?" And then she added, "Anne, the quote is from *Macbeth*, in case you don't know." (I have little formal education and little informal education.) So I read to the end of *Macbeth*—almost the end—looking for it, and I found it. Macduff hears that his wife and children have been slaughtered and he cries out, "All my pretty ones? / Did you say all? O hell-kite! All? / What! all my pretty chickens and their dam / At one fell swoop?" Later he says, "I cannot but remember such things were / That were most precious to me." Then I knew what my title was. "All My Pretty Ones" was the name for my dead. I began badly, with raw emotion and bitterness, with no good lines at all and no form, nothing but the need to give reality to feeling. So the first page goes thusly, and I apologize for the roughness but I thought people might like to see how rough it can be. What I did was roll the blank sheet into my typewriter and sit there and look at it. Here it goes.

> Somehow, God knows why, you died
> last week

Then I go down two spaces.

> Somehow, God knows how,
> I'm the only parent now.

> On the June morning they put
> my two young parents

That's no good. I go down three spaces.

God knows, it's queer enough
to have them gone

I don't like that. I go down five spaces.

Father, the worst is over,
the boozey rich man that you were

Well, I kind of like that but it isn't right yet. Down two spaces.

My mother's ashes waited
patiently at the crematory
for the ground to melt

I give up and I roll that page out. I never pick up a lot of those things again.

Now, on the second page I seem to be looking at longer lines and I'm struggling away again.

Today they dug two squares in the family plot.
My parents are ashes for the ground.
It is June. At five A.M. the same old birds
move in their nests and begin to sing.

And I go down three spaces.

As if the gospel were true,
the pitying neighbors come to comfort me . . .
How they loved each other!
Now they are in heaven together.
Father, what do they know of you?
That a second shock came boiling through
your blood.

You will note that this line is picked up in the poem. I don't lose this one. Going on:

That you went just three
months after mother. They call that love?
Father, before you had the manic time

to marry that pretty widow
(you were lonely you said)
I cried against your shoulder and three
days later you were suddenly, in Gloucester, dead.

I kind of liked that, a little. I go down two spaces and continue.

Now you will never marry anyone again.
For the last time the newspaper buried you
in large print just like the other
large rich men.
It seems it ought to be against the law
to have everyone die at once.
It is the usual June morning. The birds sing.
Time itself is the fatal flaw.
And to be left . . .
that's the difficult thing.

Well, you notice how I go off. I get very prosy and far too angry. I'm still talking to myself, which is what you do when you write a poem, I'm afraid.

Now on the next page I start trying to round into form, thinking that will help me. It's not form for the sake of "hooray I can write in form," or complicated form, but one that will help me find my voice. At this point I've gotten a copy of my father's will and I have a little legal thing here. I start out "Whereas father" which I must have gotten right from the will.

Whereas father you fell suddenly

And this has a rhyme scheme. Not the one I ended up with. It goes *a b c d e, a d b c e c.*

Whereas father you fell suddenly
on June third in the expected sea air
of this unlucky year of our Lord
nineteen hundred and fifty-nine
leaving me to shuffle through another will

leaving me with your famous alcoholic tendency
to drink down with your blood your glass of wine.

You see in the poem I pick these things up later.

Leaving me to watch over this cursed share
of the residence you could not afford;
twenty pairs of shoes, half a woolen mill,
a gold key, a Cadillac, an English Ford.

I go on with the rhyme scheme, going down about seven
spaces.

And whereas the jinx rides in my head
of your father, president of the bank
who went out shrieking in a straight jacket
of you, good God the duke you tried to be,
good God the drunk you were; good God, the man
you were the day you stopped . . . sober, jinxed instead
by a second shock boiling through your head, a refugee
from a bottle for ten years, shrieking at death you sank
from your staff because you had no wife. Back set
at your daughters you turned to anyone else's plan
and now we are your sober girls in your wage bracket.

That still wasn't right. The next page is quite long and quite
repetitious. I'll read just a little bit of it. It's a different form.
In the middle it says:

leaving me, witness to your prime,
leaving before you had the time
to marry that pretty widow, Mrs. Ricker,
(you were lonely you said)
I cried, grew disobedient, sicker
and three days later you were dead.

Then it goes on, with a different rhyme scheme, but it still
isn't right. The next page says at the top "All My Pretty
Ones." You see, I must have gotten the letter and read *Mac-
beth*. I start off this way:

Whereas father

I'm still hung up on that "whereas."

Whereas father, the jinx rides us apart

Now I have the rhyme scheme, *a b, a b c d, c d, e e*. It doesn't make any difference what rhyme scheme it is; it's what it will do for what you're trying to say.

Whereas father, the jinx rides us apart
where you followed mother to her cold slumber;
a second shock boiling its stone to your heart,
leaving me here to shuffle and disencumber
you from the residence you could not afford:
a gold key, your half of a woolen mill,
twenty pairs of shoes, an English Ford,
the love and legal verbiage of another will,
a box of picture albums that must go,
filled with nameless folk whom I do not know.

You see I'm beginning to get it, but look at that ending! That's terrible! Now the next page: it goes on, "All My Pretty Ones." I always start all over again to get the feeling. The only thing that is different now from the final version is that I changed "twenty pair of shoes" to "twenty suits from Dunne's." I drop the "whereas" and it goes this way:

Father, this year's jinx rides us apart
where you followed our mother to her cold slumber;
a second shock boiling its stone to your heart,
leaving me here to shuffle and disencumber
you from the residence you could not afford:
a gold key, your half of a woolen mill,
twenty suits from Dunne's, an English Ford,
the love and legal verbiage of another will,
boxes of pictures of people I do not know.
I touch their cardboard faces. They must go.

And that's how it began. That's all I will say. Are you there?

Moore: Yes, that's a very interesting presentation. And now,
we will have questions from the different colleges in rotation.

All My Pretty Ones

Father, this year's jinx rides us apart
where you followed our mother to her cold slumber;
a second shock boiling its stone to your heart,
leaving me here to shuffle and disencumber
you from the residence you could not afford:
a gold key, your half of a woolen mill,
twenty suits from Dunne's, an English Ford,
the love and legal verbiage of another will,
boxes of pictures of people I do not know.
I touch their cardboard faces. They must go.

But the eyes, as thick as wood in this album,
hold me. I stop here, where a small boy
waits in a ruffled dress for someone to come . . .
for this soldier who holds his bugle like a toy
or for this velvet lady who cannot smile.
Is this your father's father, this commodore
in a mailman suit? My father, time meanwhile
has made it unimportant who you are looking for.
I'll never know what these faces are all about.
I lock them into their book and throw them out.

This is the yellow scrapbook that you began
the year I was born; as crackling now and wrinkly
as tobacco leaves: clippings where Hoover outran
the Democrats, wiggling his dry finger at me
and Prohibition; news where the *Hindenburg* went
down and recent years where you went flush
on war. This year, solvent but sick, you meant
to marry that pretty widow in a one-month rush.
But before you had that second chance, I cried
on your fat shoulder. Three days later you died.

These are the snapshots of marriage, stopped in places.
Side by side at the rail toward Nassau now;
here, with the winner's cup at the speedboat races,

here, in tails at the Cotillion, you take a bow,
here, by our kennel of dogs with their pink eyes,
running like show-bred pigs in their chain-link pen;
here, at the horseshow where my sister wins a prize;
and here, standing like a duke among groups of men.
Now I fold you down, my drunkard, my navigator,
my first lost keeper, to love or look at later.

I hold a five-year diary that my mother kept
for three years, telling all she does not say
of your alcoholic tendency. You overslept,
she writes. My God, father, each Christmas Day
with your blood, will I drink down your glass
of wine? The diary of your hurly-burly years
goes to my shelf to wait for my age to pass.
Only in this hoarded span will love persevere.
Whether you are pretty or not, I outlive you,
bend down my strange face to yours and forgive you.

Stephens: You've done so beautifully in getting us into the first stanza that I hate to jump to the last line, but one of my students asks, in "All My Pretty Ones" is your "strange face" strange to him because you have not yet achieved the understanding of the age to come?

Sexton: Yes, I think so. I think that's exactly right. I think I am very much of a stranger at this point. It even reflects his strange face, you see. My strange face is my condition, my present. You know, suddenly, as I said in one of the versions, I am a parent now. *My* strange face.

Stephens: You are strange to him?

Sexton: Yes. And to myself; I would say it's also got a kind of sexual thing there. You can understand that; you know, to kiss him then, to kiss death itself. My *strange* face. It was always pretty strange to him. Only now was I trying to love him, and to forgive him for actually not being pretty.

Tougaloo: In the second stanza, about your father's old pictures, are you saying that the past of a dead person is of no use to the living, or has to be remade in some way?

Sexton: Well, it has to be remade insofar as it's useful. As I was looking at this picture album I didn't know who everyone was. There was no one left to ask. You see? I didn't know. Who was this little boy? Was it my father? I think so. Was that my father's father? I didn't know. They can't be of use to me. It was too late to ask. So I say, "they are no use to the living."

Tougaloo: And they must go.

Sexton: They must go, yes.

Drury: [. . .]Mrs. Sexton, you spoke, in your comments on this poem, to the effect that what was wrong with some of the first drafts was that you were talking to yourself. One of the controversies in twentieth-century literature has to do with the personal character of so much of our literature. One of the students is wondering if you would comment upon the personal quality of your poetry and upon the general controversy.

Sexton: Well, my poetry is very personal (*laughing*). I don't think I write public poems. I write very personal poems but I hope that they will become the central theme to someone else's private life. This is a very personal poem, of course; I bring in all these intimate details. But I hope that I give it a rather authentic stamp; that's always my hope. It's hard to defend writing this way when you can't write any other way, you see. The writer is stuck with what he can do. Any public poem I have ever written, that wasn't personal, was usually a failure. Does that answer the question at all?

Drury: Yes, it does. Thank you.

Jackson: In the third stanza you say "But before you had that second chance, I cried on your fat shoulder." Was there any special significance to the word "fat" or were you just being descriptive?

Sexton: Well, he did have fat shoulders and I think I loved him for it. I believe I was being descriptive. I don't think it had any other meaning.

Morehouse: I have a question concerning your technique. I notice that you list details one after another which seem to add up, not only to an image, but to evoke emotion. Would you care to comment on whether or not this is an operational technique in all of your poetry. What are you trying to accomplish by piling them up in that way?

Sexton: I think a feeling of authenticity, that this is real. That's exactly what I'm trying to do.

Morehouse: Are they also to carry some kind of emotional weight?

Sexton: Yes. Well, I think they gather up. You know, it is like piling stones one on top of the other.

Morehouse: So in your description of the snapshots we are to get not only a vision of the snapshots themselves, but we are also to understand how they refer to the father?

Sexton: That's right, exactly. And you feel the very weight of them, the weight of throwing such a thing out, you see. If you don't pile them up, how else do you reveal the very heaviness of them to the reader?

Langston: Mrs. Sexton, in the first stanza you said, "leaving me here to shuffle and disencumber / you from the residence you could not afford." Then, in the third stanza, you say, "this year, solvent but sick, you meant / to marry that pretty widow in a one-month rush." Is that a contradiction?

Sexton: Well, he couldn't afford it, but he was solvent. I realize I'm drawing a rather fine line there. "Solvent but sick" means going down the drain a little bit, but solvent in the world's eyes, anyway. Did I answer that? I have a feeling I didn't.

Langston: He was not really poor.

Sexton: No, he wasn't poor. Look at all the money he was spending. But he couldn't really afford all these things. It was madness to spend money this lavishly, but he was solvent.

Moore: Stephens, would you like something further on this?

Stephens: We'd like to follow up the question from Drury, asking about the personal quality. One of the criticisms that we hear of contemporary poetry is that it is so academic. One of the great values of Mrs. Sexton's poetry is that it is personal. Through this personal quality we feel what has generally been described as universality. Are you making a conscious effort to get back to basic elements or is this simply the only way, as you say, you can do it?

Sexton: I think it's just my style. I think if I had written twenty years ago I'd have written this way, whether it were stylish, whether it were a good thing to do or a bad thing to do. I can just do my own thing and that's the way I do it. I have been quite aware of criticism about this, naturally, because I do it; but I can't seem to change. I don't think I'm aiming at anything from an intellectual standpoint. I didn't make up my mind to write personal poems. When I started to write everyone told me, "These are too personal. These should not be published. You can't write that way." I tried to make them better poems, but they still had to be just my kind of poems. You might call it an accident.

Stephens: Don't change them at all. Don't listen to what they say.

Sexton (laughter): I can't. [. . .]

Tougaloo: In the last stanza, the middle section: "My God, father, each Christmas Day / with your blood, will I drink down your glass / of wine?" Could you comment on that? I noticed it occurred in one of your earlier drafts.

Sexton: Yes, I think I mean will I inherit this . . . Christmas Day is a day of great celebration, you know, and I feel with his blood, which, in a way, is contaminated, in a way, is beautiful—will I drink down the same glass? In a way I am asking, will I inherit your glass, your wine, and your tendency. Just preceding it I say, "telling all she does not say / of your alcoholic tendency. You overslept, / she writes. My God, father" Where will I do this? When will this happen to me?

Tougaloo: Are the blood and the wine fused?

Sexton: Yes, I think so. I'm sure that no poet can say they weren't.

Stephens: This is a reference to the sacrament?

Sexton: Very likely. Only on an unconscious level. You just can't get away from it, you see.

Stephens: And your father becomes you?

Sexton: That's right.

Morehouse: The diary comes in in a strange way. One student asks, if you see your father's life so realistically and poetically at the same time, why this sudden shift to the diary which seems to be a repeated censuring of his nature?

Sexton: Well, because I am cataloging these leftover objects and the diary was of a time past that I lived through, you know. But these were bad years. They tell of the worst in him.

Morehouse: Then would it be a comment on the mother's reaction to the father?

Sexton: Of course, of course. And the family's reaction. But what Mother put down was not really the truth; it was a euphemism. And reading through the diary I thought, "Where did this happen?" and yet I would only read "He overslept." Her saying that personified the alcoholism. The worst of him.

Morehouse: Is there any relationship in the poem between the expenditure of the money and the alcoholism? Are we supposed to see this as a cause and effect relationship?

Sexton: I don't think so. I think that's too simple, too pat an explanation.

Langston: Did your opposition to your father's marriage have anything to do with his death?

Sexton: Of course I felt that. Not rationally, but I felt it. It's not, perhaps, as implicit as I hoped, but in the poem I don't want him to marry and then he dies. It's kind of Oedipal or something, but it's distinctly there, my guilt. [. . .]

Stephens: I would be interested in further comment on that last point. Mrs. Sexton's poet's guilt might be there but this question pointed to a direct relationship and I don't think that was intended, was it?

Sexton (silence): I'm thinking. Yes, I think a direct relationship.

Stephens: A direct relationship.

Sexton: Well, somewhat. Certainly the act makes it direct anyway.

The Division of Parts

1.
Mother, my Mary Gray,
once resident of Gloucester
and Essex County,
a photostat of your will
arrived in the mail today.
This is the division of money.
I am one third
of your daughters counting my bounty
or I am a queen alone
in the parlor still,
eating the bread and honey.
It is Good Friday.
Black birds pick at my window sill.

Your coat in my closet,
your bright stones on my hand,
the gaudy fur animals
I do not know how to use,
settle on me like a debt.
A week ago, while the hard March gales
beat on your house,
we sorted your things: obstacles
of letters, family silver,
eyeglasses and shoes.
Like some unseasoned Christmas, its scales
rigged and reset,
I bundled out with gifts I did not choose.

Now the hours of The Cross
rewind. In Boston, the devout
work their cold knees
toward that sweet martyrdom
that Christ planned. My timely loss
is too customary to note; and yet
I planned to suffer
and I cannot. It does not please
my yankee bones to watch

where the dying is done
in its ugly hours. Black birds peck
at my window glass
and Easter will take its ragged son.

The clutter of worship
that you taught me, Mary Gray,
is old. I imitate
a memory of belief
that I do not own. I trip
on your death and Jesus, *my stranger*
floats up over
my Christian home, wearing his straight
thorn tree. I have cast my lot
and am one third thief
of you. Time, that rearranger
of estates, equips
me with your garments, but not with grief.

2.
This winter when
cancer began its ugliness
I grieved with you each day
for three months
and found you in your private nook
of the medicinal palace
for New England Women
and never once
forgot how long it took.

I read to you
from *The New Yorker,* ate suppers
you wouldn't eat, fussed
with your flowers,
joked with your nurses, as if I
were the balm among lepers,
as if I could undo
a life in hours
if I never said goodbye.

But you turned old,
all your fifty-eight years sliding

like masks from your skull;
and at the end
I packed your nightgowns in suitcases,
paid the nurses, came riding
home as if I'd been told
I could pretend
people live in places.

3.
Since then I have pretended ease,
loved with the trickeries of need, but not enough
to shed my daughterhood
or sweeten him as a man.
I drink the five o'clock martinis
and poke at this dry page like a rough
goat. Fool! I fumble my lost childhood
for a mother and lounge in sad stuff
with love to catch and catch as catch can.

And Christ still waits. I have tried
to exorcise the memory of each event
and remain still, a mixed child,
heavy with cloths of you.
Sweet witch, you are my worried guide.
Such dangerous angels walk through Lent.
Their walls creak *Anne! Convert! Convert!*
My desk moves. Its cave murmurs Boo
and I am taken and beguiled.

Or wrong. For all the way I've come
I'll have to go again. Instead, I must convert
to love as reasonable
as Latin, as solid as earthenware:
an equilibrium
I never knew. And Lent will keep its hurt
for someone else. Christ knows enough
staunch guys have hitched on him in trouble,
thinking his sticks were badges to wear.

4.
Spring rusts on its skinny branch
and last summer's lawn

is soggy and brown.
Yesterday is just a number.
All of its winters avalanche
out of sight. What was, is gone.
Mother, last night I slept
in your Bonwit Teller nightgown.
Divided, you climbed into my head.
There in my jabbering dream
I heard my own angry cries
and I cursed you, *Dame*
keep out of my slumber.
My good Dame, you are dead.
And Mother, three stones
slipped from your glittering eyes.

Now it is Friday's noon
and I would still curse
you with my rhyming words
and bring you flapping back, old love,
old circus knitting, god-in-her-moon,
all fairest in my lang syne verse,
the gauzy bride among the children,
the fancy amid the absurd
and awkward, that horn for hounds
that skipper homeward, that museum
keeper of stiff starfish, that blaze
within the pilgrim woman,
a clown mender, a dove's
cheek among the stones,
my Lady of my first words,
this is the division of ways.

And now, while Christ stays
fastened to his Crucifix
so that love may praise
his sacrifice
and not the grotesque metaphor,
you come, a brave ghost, to fix
in my mind without praise
or paradise
to make me your inheritor.

Stephens: We will go to "The Division of Parts." One of the main things is the use of religious symbolism.

Sexton: I'll do my best.

Stephens: If you could just comment generally about it then maybe others will have questions.

Sexton: I'd rather have questions. Well, what I did was spend a long time reading over the New Testament. I guess I had a lot of religious feeling—it was this Good Friday thing—it was the whole act of sorting out my mother's possessions. I don't know how my mother could have become like Christ to me, but I got it all mixed up. And, you see, I felt like the soldier who divided Christ's garments and I used this. That led me into this religious symbolism. A poet doesn't just say, "Well now, I'm going to speak in symbols," you know. It just gets all enmeshed in your mind and you try to feel your way through it. I even have a nursery rhyme. It's in there too.

Stephens (laughter): Yes, I wonder if you would comment on "the blackbirds."

Sexton: Yes. Well, you know, "I am the queen alone in the parlor still" goes with it, and "the king is in the counting house counting out the money, the queen is in the parlor eating bread and honey." The maid is—I don't know where she is—but hanging out the clothes and the blackbird, I don't know that it exactly bites off her nose, but this was the ominous symbol. "I am the queen alone in the parlor still," means I have inherited all these material goods.

Stephens: The clothes are in the closet, aren't they?

Sexton: That's right.

Tougaloo: We would like to pick up this question of the symbolism. You present your mother and Christ as very similar and yet different. Could you comment more fully on their relationship?

Sexton: You mean on how they are alike?

Tougaloo: Yes. Well, alike and different.

Sexton: Well, I don't think I fully saw how different they were until the end of the poem when I realized it was a very bad metaphor. But to me, my mother's long suffering—(pause) I didn't want to believe, you see. I didn't want to believe in Christ rising. I didn't want to believe in anything. I felt that I had inherited all these things—I cast my lot—I had gotten them all: the division of parts, the division of money, and all that she had gone through. I say, "I trip / on your death and Jesus, my stranger / my Christian home." Jesus was a stranger to me and I trip always on this death, her death, as in the resurrection. And then, of course, on Good Friday Jesus is on the cross and I am speaking of this.

Drury: One of our students is interested in the division image as it occurs in the fourth section of the poem where you say "Divided, you climbed into my head" and then at the end the "division of ways." Could you explain this a little more?

Sexton (pause): Divided at this point between life and death, I think, when she climbs into my head. She has been divided because I have divided her. She has been divided into three parts. She is now just her three daughters and I am one part of this division. Then I think by the division of ways I mean the parting, that I must go my own way and Christ must stay where he is and I must be the inheritor. It comes to an acceptance of the division.

Jackson: This may have been answered, but I would like to ask it. Does the poem imply that the dead mother is symbolic of

Christ in that they both left legacies? Also is there the idea that the inheritor took the material gifts that were left by her mother but not the spiritual gifts that her mother tried to instill in her?

Sexton: Exactly. A very good question, well put. I'm not sure that I was consciously aware of this analogy.

Morehouse: We have a question about the third section. We'll try first the general approach. Just what is the meaning of the third section? That has caused us some confusion also.

Sexton: Well, "Since then I have pretended ease" because I have tried to live, to go on with my life; to live with need, but not enough to shed the daughterhood, nor to sweeten him as a man. That's the regular life going on. I'm not succeeding at being a woman at this point. I am still poking at this dry page and trying to write this poem that will exorcise my feeling, fumbling for a childhood, catching at love. But Christ is still waiting and I haven't gotten over my loss. I haven't succeeded in continuing. I bring in this section because it is part of living.

Morehouse: Our second question concerns the witch image and the "*Convert! Convert!*" Is that your mother calling to you in some remembered past?

Sexton: Possibly. She could call, or Christ might call through her in some way that the dead can speak back, that I would be converted to the magic of the resurrection.

Morehouse: Finally, are you perhaps the persons of the poem, one of the blackbirds in a kind of inverse sense, in the sense of despair, and guilt and shame sort of mixed together?

Sexton: I doubt it. I think the blackbirds are really a symbol of evil. In some way, in my mind, they are tied up with the cross.

They seem to me almost like the nails of the cross, a very dark omen.

Langston: Will you explain the symbolism in section four, the last lines of the first stanza.

Sexton: "*My good Dame, you are dead.* And Mother, three stones"—is that what you mean?

Langston: Yes.

Sexton: Her tears have become stones. This is my way of facing the very deadness of her body. Then I say, get out of here, get out of my dreams, you are dead! But then, almost in horror, I see that three stones slip from her eyes, as though she were crying. At this point she becomes almost as beautiful as Mary, after I have sworn at her. Does that answer the question?

Langston: Yes, thank you.

Moore: Our time is going all too rapidly in this wonderful session. Now, a question from Stephens College.

Stephens: You say about the last three lines of stanza one of part four, this is almost like the Virgin. Then you pick it up in "my Lady of my first words"?

Sexton: That's right. That's right.

Stephens: This is a part of the same image?

Sexton: Yes.

Stephens: In terms of the time of composition did this precede "All My Pretty Ones" by any great number of weeks or months?

Sexton: Oh yes. By four months. When I wrote "Division of Parts" my father had not died.

Stephens: We wondered at picking up "Dame" in that section; the relation of this to the quotation from *Macbeth*.

Sexton: No, I hadn't read it. You see I was writing this on Good Friday and my mother was recently dead. My father didn't die until June and I didn't read *Macbeth* until then.

I Remember

By the first of August
the invisible beetles began
to snore and the grass was
as tough as hemp and was
no color—no more than
the sand was a color and
we had worn our bare feet
bare since the twentieth
of June and there were times
we forgot to wind up your
alarm clock and some nights
we took our gin warm and neat
from old jelly glasses while
the sun blew out of sight
like a red picture hat and
one day I tied my hair back
with a ribbon and you said
that I looked almost like
a puritan lady and what
I remember best is that
the door to your room was
the door to mine.

Moore: Tougaloo, do you want to ask a question about "I Remember"?

Tougaloo: Yes. We would like to discuss the punctuation in this poem. Did you *not* use punctuation to show the continuity of things during the period you are talking about or were there other more formal reasons?

Sexton: I'll tell you exactly why I did it this way. I feel both this and "Young," although this even more, are supposed to be breathless poems. Of course it's not possible, they should be said in *one breath.* They are each one sentence because I only try to capture an instant in them, where in other poems I try to cover vast amounts of time, to tie things together. In this I just want to take a photograph and that's all I want. So it's just a run-on; it's a gathering. The only important thing are the last three lines really. That is why I used no punctuation. It's supposed to be thin, like a tube.

Moore: Thank you. Drury College, do you want to ask questions on "I Remember" and/or "Young"?

Young

A thousand doors ago
when I was a lonely kid
in a big house with four
garages and it was summer
as long as I could remember,
I lay on the lawn at night,
clover wrinkling under me,
the wise stars bedding over me,
my mother's window a funnel
of yellow heat running out,
my father's window, half shut,
an eye where sleepers pass,
and the boards of the house
were smooth and white as wax
and probably a million leaves
sailed on their strange stalks
as the crickets ticked together
and I, in my brand new body,
which was not a woman's yet,
told the stars my questions

and thought God could really see
the heat and the painted light,
elbows, knees, dreams, goodnight.

Drury: One of the students asked that Mrs. Sexton give us a reading of one or the other of these that we might hear how she reads it.

Sexton: I'd love to. Shall I do it?

Moore: Please do.

Sexton: I'll read "I Remember." Now you're going to catch me because I don't read it the way it's written. But that's all right; it's good to catch poets. (Mrs. Sexton reads "I Remember.") That's the way it's supposed to be read.

Drury: Thank you very much.

Morehouse: We would like to ask a question about "Young" if we can also go back to "The Division of Parts." In "Young" there is this reference to "my mother's window a funnel / of yellow heat running out, / my father's window, . . ." We note a strange ambiguity of your grief in "The Division of Parts." We feel that it is ambiguity because of the double feeling you seem to be having toward your mother. Does this grow out of this past reference to the Freudian symbolism here in this line?

Sexton: I think so, yes.

Morehouse: Then, is this a part of your dynamic? In "The Division of Parts" is the kind of guilt that you feel being unable to grieve?

Sexton: Exactly, exactly. That's why you keep writing these poems.

Moore: Back to Stephens College. Do you want to take up "Flight"?

Flight

Thinking that I would find you,
thinking I would make the plane
that goes hourly out of Boston
I drove into the city.
Thinking that on such a night
every thirsty man would have his jug
and that the Negro women would lie down
on pale sheets and even the river into town
would stretch out naturally on its couch,
I drove into the city.
On such a night, at the end of the river,
the airport would sputter with planes
like ticker-tape.

Foot on the gas
I sang aloud to the front seat,
to the clumps of women in cotton dresses,
to the patches of fog crusting the banks,
and to the sailboats swinging on their expensive hooks.
There was rose and violet on the river
as I drove through the mist into the city.
I was full of letters I hadn't sent you,
a red coat over my shoulders
and new white gloves in my lap.

I dropped through the city
as the river does,
rumbling over and under, as indicated,
past the miles of spotted windows
minding their own business,
through the Sumner Tunnel,
trunk by trunk through its sulphurous walls,
tile by tile like a men's urinal,
slipping through
like somebody else's package.

Parked, at last,
on a dime that would never last,
I ran through the airport.
Wild for love, I ran through the airport,
stockings and skirts and dollars.

The night clerk yawned all night at the public,
his mind on tomorrow's wages.
All flights were grounded.
The planes sat and the gulls sat,
heavy and rigid in a pool of glue.

Knowing I would never find you
I drove out of the city.
At the airport one thousand cripples
sat nursing a sore foot.
There was more fog
and the rain came down when it thought of it.
I drove past the eye and ear infirmaries,
past the office buildings lined up like dentures,
and along Storrow Drive the streetlights
sucked in all the insects who
had nowhere else to go.

Stephens: The last three lines of "Flight" seem to have a mixture of qualities of conflicting natures—generosity, despair,
loneliness—are we correct in assuming that at the end of this
poem you too feel that you have "nowhere else to go"?

Sexton: Of course, and I don't think there's much generosity
in it, except the image, the impulse to fly and then it becomes
more and more depersonalized. It's sort of an image, "one
thousand cripples / sat nursing a sore foot." They're frozen.
And then I go past the eye and ear infirmaries, and buildings
like dentures, all false, and then along the drive the streetlights suck in all the insects who have nowhere else to go just
as I am sucked in, I have nowhere else to go. That is the very
point in that image.

Stephens: And if we could have one last question then. Do you feel that the sea and the whole New England element are important to you in the creative process?

Sexton: Yes. But that's because I happen to live right near the sea and love it. I think if I had grown up beside a cornfield it would have become very much a part of me; or the flatlands. Your region becomes imbedded in you.

Moore: Tougaloo College, on "Flight"?

Tougaloo: Yes. There are a number of rather startling similes in this poem, especially when you look at them at the ends of stanzas or the ends of lines and in some of your other poems too. Does your mind work this way, rather particularly with similes?

Sexton: Yes, I think so. I think something that is more dissimilar is more shocking, brings you closer to the reality, the intensification, of the feeling. I have a great love of ending a stanza with a kind of "pulled up" effect. This poem has no rhyme. Sometimes you can tie things together with rhyme and if you're not using it then you must use other methods.

Jackson: Just a general question: Is it implied in this poem that the adolescent is trying to reach out for understanding and not finding it in mother or father?

Sexton: You mean in "Young"? No, because I think that the adolescent just glances at the windows, those strange windows or strange people. No, it's lying on the ground and asking questions of yourself. I would say the key lines are, "and I, in my brand new body, / which was not a woman's yet, / told the

stars my questions." You see, it's this feeling of being out-
doors and wondering, of thinking suddenly, "why I'm alive!"
Your parents are very far away. [. . .]

With Patricia Marx

I understand that you started writing poetry only in 1957. What made you begin at such a late date?

Well, it was actually personal experience, because I had had a nervous breakdown, and as I was recovering I started to write, and I got more and more serious about it, and I started out writing almost a poem a day. It was a kind of rebirth at twenty-nine.

What do you think caused you to write poetry after a breakdown? What was the impetus?

It's too strange. It's just a matter of coincidence. I think probably I'm an artist at heart, and I've found my own form, which I think is poetry. I was looking at educational television in Boston, and I. A. Richards was explaining the form of a sonnet, and I thought, "Well, so that's a sonnet." Although I had learned it in high school, I hadn't ever done anything about it. And so I thought, "I'll try that, too. I think maybe I could." So I sat down and wrote in the form of the sonnet. I was so pleased with myself that for about three months I wrote a sonnet every day. There are no sonnets in my book. They have since been discarded. But that's the way I started.

Reprinted by permission from the *Hudson Review* 18, no. 4 (Winter, 1965/66). Copyright © 1966 by The Hudson Review, Inc.

When did you start taking yourself seriously as a poet?

I think when I was published. After I'd been writing about a year and a half I started sending things to magazines, and collecting rejection slips. I wasted a lot of time on it. There were kind of two sides of me. One part was writing poems very seriously and the other was running this little fool's business, which meant I will send out my poems today to four magazines, and the mail will bring five or six poems back.

You often mention your experience in an asylum where you wrote poetry. Did you write when you were very disturbed, or afterwards? Did you find writing had a beneficial effect on your health?

I don't think so particularly. It certainly did not create mental health. It isn't as simple as my poetry makes it, because I simplified everything to make it more dramatic. I have written poems in a mental institution, but only later, not at the beginning.

There is a popular notion that creative genius is very close to insanity. Many of our major poets now, such as Robert Lowell and Theodore Roethke before he died, often had mental breakdowns. Do you feel there's truth in this notion?

Well, their genius is more important than their disease. I think there are so many people who are mentally disturbed who are not writers, or artists, or painters or whatever, that I don't think genius and insanity grow in the same bed. I think the artist must have a heightened awareness. It is only seldom this sprouts from mental illness alone. However, there *is* this great feeling of heightened awareness that all artists must have.

In your book, All My Pretty Ones, *you quote this part of a letter written by Franz Kafka: "The books we need are the kind that act upon us like a misfortune, that make us suffer like the death of someone we love more than ourselves. . . . a book should serve as the axe for the frozen sea within us." Is this the purpose you want your poetry to serve?*

Absolutely. I feel it should do that. I think it should be a shock to the senses. It should almost hurt.

Do you find that all poetry does this when you read it? Do you admire certain poetry more for doing this?

No, not necessarily. I think it's just my little declaration to myself. I put it in the book to show the reader what I felt, but Kafka's work certainly works upon me as an axe upon a frozen sea. But I admire many poets, many writers who don't do this.

I wonder if you would further explain that metaphor.

I see it very literally as an axe, cutting right through a slab of ice. I think we go along very complacently and are brainwashed with all kinds of pablum, advertisements every minute, the sameness of supermarkets, everything—it's not only the modern world, even trees become trite—and we need something to shock us, to make us become more aware. It doesn't need to happen in such a shocking way, perhaps, as in my poetry. I think of the poetry of Elizabeth Bishop, which seems to have beautiful ordered clarity. Her fish hurts as much as Randall Jarrell's speaking people. They are two of my favorite poets. Their work shocks me into being more alive, and that's maybe what I mean. The poet doesn't have to use my method to have that happen to me. And Rilke, think of Rilke with his depth, his terrible pain!—

Do you find that the writing of poetry achieves this for you as well as the reading of it?

No, the writing actually puts things back in place. I mean, things are more chaotic, and if I can write a poem, I come into order again, and the world is again a little more sensible, and real. I'm more in touch with things.

How does a poem come into being?

Oh, that's a terrible question! I don't know. Sometimes you get a line, a phrase, sometimes you're crying, or it's the curve of a chair that hurts you and you don't know why, or sometimes you just want to write a poem, and you don't know what it's about. I will fool around on the typewriter. It might take me ten pages of nothing, of terrible writing, and then I'll get a line, and I'll think, "That's what I mean!" What you're doing is hunting for what you mean, what you're trying to say. You don't know when you start.

Do you work on it a long time?

I work on it a very long time. For one lyric poem I rewrote about three hundred typewritten pages. Often I keep my worksheets, so that once in a while when I get depressed and think that I'll never write again, I can go back and see how that poem came into being. You watch the work and you watch the miracle. You have to look back at all those bad words, bad metaphors, everything started wrong, and then see how it came into being, the slow progress of it, because you're always fighting to find out what it is that you want to say. You have to go deeper and deeper each time. You wonder why you didn't drown at the time—deeper and deeper.

Is it a struggle or pleasure?

Oh, it's a wonderful pleasure. It's a struggle, but there's great happiness in working. As anyone knows, if you're doing something that you love and you're struggling with it, there's happiness there, particularly if you can get it in the end. And I'm pretty stubborn. I need to keep after it, until I get it. Or I keep after it until I kill it.

Do you discard many poems that you write?

Well, now I think I prediscard them. I don't write them, which is one reason why I write less than I did in the beginning. I wrote a lot of unimportant poems, and now when I look at a poem, I always wonder why was this written. There should be a reason for it. It should do something to me. It should move me. I have some poems that have haunted me for four or five years, and they're unfinished and maybe they'll never be finished. I know they're not right, but it hurts not to write them. I have this great need somehow to keep that time of my life, that feeling. I want to imprison it in a poem, to keep it. It's almost in a way like keeping a scrapbook to make life mean something as it goes by, to rescue it from chaos—to make "now" last.

In your first volume of poetry, To Bedlam and Part Way Back, *you quote another passage from a letter, this time from Schopenhauer to Goethe, and it says, "It is the courage to make a clean breast of it in face of every question that makes the philosopher." I take it that you mean this courage also makes a poet.*

Yes, exactly. It's very hard to reveal yourself. Frankly, anything I say to you is useless and probably more deceiving than revealing. I tell so much truth in my poetry that I'm a fool if I say any more. To really get at the truth of something is the poem, not the poet.

Do you find that you are more truthful in your poetry than you are to yourself?

Yes, I think so. That's what I'm hunting for when I'm working away there in the poem. I'm hunting for the truth. It might be a kind of poetic truth, and not just a factual one, because behind everything that happens to you, every act, there is another truth, a secret life.

You wrote for the Poetry Book Society, "All poets lie. As I said once in a poem, a writer is essentially a crook. With used furniture he makes a tree." Now how do you reconcile that with your remark about poetry being the truth?

I think maybe it's an evasion of mine. It's a very easy thing to say, "All poets lie." It depends on what you want to call the truth, you see, and it's also a way of getting out of the literal fact of a poem. You can say there is truth in this, but it might not be the truth of my experience. Then again, if you say that you lie, you can get away with telling the awful truth. That's why it's an evasion. The poem counts for more than your life.

Do you find that you often distort the literal facts of your life to present the emotional truth that lies under them?

Well, I think this is necessary. It's something that an artist must do to make it clear and dramatic and to have the effect of the axe. To have that effect you must distort some of these facts to give them their own clarity. As an easy example, in my long poem to my daughter and about my mental illness, I don't imply that I was ever in an institution more than once, but that was the dramatic truth. The actual truth was something quite different. I returned quite a few times, and the fact that I have two children was not mentioned in this, because the dramatic point was I had one child, and was writing to her. It made it a better poem to distort it this way. I just don't mention it. So you don't have to include everything to tell the truth. You can exclude many things. You can even lie (one can confess and lie forever) as I did in the poem of the illegitimate child that the girl had to give up. It hadn't happened to me. It wasn't true, and yet it was indeed the truth.

Are you the ultimate judge of what the truth is?

No. There's the trouble. No, I'm not.

What is the criterion?

I don't think there is one. I mean, people lie to themselves so much—postmarks lie, even gravestones lie. The effort is to try to get to some form of integrity when you write a poem, some whole life lived, to try to present it now, to give the impact. It's the same as with a novelist, only it's in little sections.

Are you ever influenced, or do you ever learn anything from critics?

Oh, they're very disturbing. I don't know what I learn. I just want to say, "Gee whiz, kids, that's the best way I could do it," something like that. One prolific poet whom I greatly admire can hardly write a damning review without mentioning my name in connection with "mechanically bad writing." What should I do? Send him a telegram? I carried one very bad review in my wallet all over Europe. The good reviews I left at home. But even over there I was still Anne. I couldn't change her. I think mostly reviewers are upsetting. You just love the praise, and you try to shut out the criticism. I don't know how much they can influence you. I don't think they always read you correctly, but you always think the ones that like you are reading you pretty well.

Very few women have been great poets. Do you find that there's a difficulty in being a woman and a creative artist?

I think they are really very closely allied. I don't think it's that difficult at all. It's within a woman to create, to make order, to be an emotional, full human being. I think; perhaps men are better because they are denied this in their lives. Therefore they put more of it into a poem, and maybe if you are born with an extra amount, as a woman, it works out all right. You have enough for life itself, you have a family, and then you have some left over. It always seems to me I have too much left over. Maybe that's an ingredient.

In one of your poems, "The Black Art," you wrote, "A woman who writes feels too much, those trances and portents" and then in another stanza, "A man who writes knows too much, such spells and fetiches." Do you think there is this distinction between the woman being the feeling creature and the man being the rational?

I don't think so, really. I think I was lying a little bit. It is in that same poem I said a writer is essentially a crook, and we're quite together in that, the male and female. I don't think that man is the rational being, and there are some marvelous women poets who are very rational: Marianne Moore, Elizabeth Bishop. May Swenson is a very good poet and certainly not overemotional in any way. She knows just when to hold back and when to give forth. Then there are male poets who are so emotional that I don't think this holds true. Great poets know both.

You were mentioning that perhaps the reason that more men have been great poets is that they are denied the creativity that comes naturally to women, through having children. Do you think then that some kind of channeling or denial is important?

Well, it hasn't been for me. I think that it might be so. Sometimes I think, "Oh, I'm so lonely." This is the curse of being a writer or an artist, but then I think that great artists such as Rilke have treasured this, worshipped this. And then sometimes I think I'd give it all up if I could just be comfortable and with things. I think women are essentially *with* things. They're part of the earth, and perhaps it's my own peculiar trait that I feel not part of the earth. Therefore I look at it a little more sharply. I feel a little more outcast, and it perhaps makes me more of a writer.

That may be the dilemma of the modern woman, though—

Oh, I don't know! Poor modern woman!

What is your feeling about the "feminine mystique"? One is always hearing of the problems of modern woman. Do you think it's any worse now?

Maybe modern woman is more conscious now, more thinking. I can't tell. Sometimes I feel like another creature, hardly a woman, although I certainly am, in my life. I can't be a modern woman. I'm a Victorian teenager—at heart. I noticed in Europe that women are not complaining as much, and their lives are certainly not as good as ours. We have much more freedom, and we can speak up, and I like that. I like to speak up.

You mentioned before that as a writer you feel alone and not part of the earth.

It isn't as a writer. It's as a human being.

Do you feel you are associated with any other poets?

I am often likened to Robert Lowell or W. D. Snodgrass, and I think we all kind of got born into this about the same time, writing in a certain frank style. I do find that perhaps I'm drawn to women poets because some of them have some quality that I lack. I often find myself liking a poet, for example, May Swenson, or Elizabeth Bishop, who does something that I can't do at all, and I admire it for being so clear and true and having a beauty that doesn't seem to shine from my poetry at all. I don't feel as though I'm part of any group, because I'm too much off by myself, and not in the academic world, except that I did study with Robert Lowell for a while.

I wonder in what way you feel his poetry influenced your work?

Actually, this is a terrible thing to admit, but I had not read any of his poetry when I studied with him. I did not go to college, and when I was studying with him I was so innocent as not to have read any of his poems, and his *Life Studies* had not come out at the time. They came out after I had finished studying with him. So they didn't influence me at all, because I hadn't seen them. If anything influenced me it was W. D. Snodgrass's *Heart's Needle*. I had written about half of my first book when I read that poem, and it moved me to such an extent—it's about a child, and he has to give up his child, which seems to be one of my themes, and I didn't have my own daughter at that time—that I ran up to my mother-in-law's where she was living and got her back. I could only keep her at that time for a week, but the poem moved me to *action*. It so changed me, and undoubtedly it must have influenced my own poetry. At the time everyone said, "You can't write this way. It's too personal; it's confessional; you can't write this, Anne," and everyone was discouraging me. But then I saw Snodgrass doing what I was doing, and it kind of gave me permission.

I wonder what is the relationship between form and making a poem function like an axe. In what way do you approach a poem stylistically and in what way does content dominate?

Content dominates, but style is the master. I think that's what makes a poet. The form is always important. To me there's something about fiction that is too large to hold. I can see a poem, even my long ones, as something you could hold, like a piece of something. It isn't that I care about the shape of it on the page, but the line must look right to me. About half of my poems are in some sort of form. The poems that aren't in form have a shape, just the same, even if it isn't a vase or anything that simple, but they have a kind of shape, a body of their own. There are some stories that are long and thin. They should be. There's a reason for it. I don't decide this. The story writes itself and must find its right form. I'm not talking about something that's particularly academic, or perhaps it is. It's just a little trick that I have of my own.

Do you mean by form just the physical look of the poem?

Yes, sometimes, but also the sound. But I think of it as something you can hold. I think of it with my hands to begin with. I

79

don't know what the poem will be and I start out writing and it looks wrong. I start a long line and that looks wrong, and a short line, and I play around with rhyme, and then I sometimes make a kind of impossible syllabic count, and if I can get the first verse and it's right, then I might keep on with that for four more verses, and then I might change it because I felt that it needed a new rhythm. It has as much to do with speech as it does with the way it will look on the page, because it will change speech—it's a kind of compression. I used to describe it this way; that if you used form it was like letting a lot of wild animals out in the arena, but enclosing them in a cage, and you could let some extraordinary animals out if you had the right cage, and that cage would be form.

In the same article that you wrote for the Poetry Book Society you said, "Form for me is a trick to deceive myself, not you, but me."

I can explain that exactly. I think all form is a trick in order to get at the truth. Sometimes in my hardest poems, the ones that are difficult to write, I might make an impossible scheme, a syllabic count that is so involved, that it then allows me to be truthful. It works as a kind of superego. It says, "You may now face it, because it will be impossible ever to get out." Almost any accomplished poet can do this. The point is can you get to the real, the sharp edge of the poem? But you see how I say this not to deceive you, but to deceive me. I deceive myself, saying to myself you can't do it, and then if I can get it, then I have deceived myself, then I can change it and do what I want. I can even change and rearrange it so no one can see my trick. It won't change what's real. It's there on paper.

Do you really set the rules to begin with?

I don't set the rules. I don't sit down and say, "I'm going to have *a b c d e* and fourteen syllables." I work and work for the first stanza, and if it looks right and if it feels right, then I cement it. I say, "Okay, here it is." I have done this with some poems. The syllabic count is this, the rhyme goes *a b c a b c* or however, and I follow that, and then after I've done it, and it's sometimes very hard, I may change it so that no one could look back over it and see that I had made this small conceit. Better to hide conceits like this and leave it raw. Take out rules and leave the instant.

And this works in your best poems?

Well, perhaps my hardest. I must say I don't do it as often now. In my newer poems I'm not using form half as much, and I don't know to what to attribute this. I don't know what it is.

By form then you really mean the physical shape of the poem and how it sounds?

And how it rhymes and the length of the lines. Sometimes a short line is a very sharp thing, and the breaking of a line, the breaking of the rhythm is a very important thing. I think of all these things quite magically, and not in some academic way, because I don't really know what my form is. With old poems I have to go back and study it like a graduate student, because I forget it, suppress it. I forget what I did, and that's why sometimes I keep these worksheets to look back and see what kind of little magical tricks I use to get to it.

Over the seven or eight years you have been writing poetry, do you feel you've developed in terms of form or style?

Well, perhaps, I would say I think the second book better written than the first and yet, in a way, I think the second lacks some of the impact and honesty of the first, which I wrote when I was so raw that I didn't know any better. In the second book I knew a little bit more about how to write, and sometimes, perhaps, I cooled it too much. I didn't let myself go enough. I think maybe this will happen in a third book, which is not finished; that there are too many poems I'm not writing, that in a way I know too much. The first book was just kind of a miracle. I don't know how it came to be. There is some very bad writing in some of my best poems, and yet those flaws seem to me to make them even better. A little more honest in their own kind of silly way. There they are with all their flaws, a little more human, you might say.

Do you find that you deal very much with the same themes? There do seem to be recurring themes throughout.

Yes, there's the mother-child theme, and death very much, although, I think, maybe a little less. Any writer, any artist I'm sure, is obsessed with death, a prerequisite for life. I'm afraid they are quite repetitive, but I think that's all right. I don't think you need too many different themes. I could defend this, not just because it seems to be what I'm doing, but in other writers that I've loved. I could defend their repetition of a theme. I would say to have written this is a wonderful thing, about some other writer, and then I try not to condemn myself for not changing a little more, although my critics like it if I change. They want to see me broaden my scope and do something different.

Do you find you come to an understanding or a peace with the problems that you're dealing with, through writing about them all the time?

Just in a very small way, a very qualified way. There is a big change after you write a poem. It's a marvelous feeling, and there's a big change in the psyche, but I think you really go into great chaos just before you write a poem, and during it, and then to have come out of that whole, somehow is a small miracle, which lasts for a couple of days. Then on to the next.

With Barbara Kevles

Pulitzer prize-winning poet Anne Sexton discovered her craft late in life. Born in 1928, she married and bore two children before she settled down to serious writing. With the publication of each book, grants and awards followed. To Bedlam and Part Way Back *(1960) led to admittance to Radcliffe's Institute for Independent Study (1961–63);* All My Pretty Ones *(1962) brought her the first traveling fellowship offered by the American Academy of Arts and Letters (1963–64), a Ford Foundation grant in playwriting (1964–65), and the first literary magazine travel grant from The Congress for Cultural Freedom (1965). That same year, her* Selected Poems *appeared in England, and she was elected Fellow of The Royal Society of Literature. Her third book,* Live or Die *(1966), won the 1967 Pulitzer Prize for Poetry and the Shelley Award from the Poetry Society of America. A fourth book,* Love Poems, *was published in 1969.*

The interview took place over three days in the middle of August, 1968. When asked about dates of publications or other events, Anne Sexton kept saying, "Let me think, I want this to be accurate." And she'd use the births of her children as reference dates to chronicle the event in question. Sometimes her distinctions between real and imagined life blurred, as in scenes from Pirandello. Often, her answers sounded like incantations, repetitious chants which if pared down would lose something of their implications, and so, for the most part,

Writers at Work: The Paris Review Interviews, 4th series, edited by George Plimpton. Copyright © 1974, 1975 by The Paris Review, Inc. Reprinted by permission of Viking Peguin Inc.

they are preserved in their entirety. Even when replying from written notes, she read with all the inflections and intonations of—as she describes her readings—"an actress in her own autobiographical play."*

You were almost thirty before you began writing poetry. Why?

Until I was twenty-eight I had a kind of buried self who didn't know she could do anything but make white sauce and diaper babies. I didn't know I had any creative depths. I was a victim of the American Dream, the bourgeois, middle-class dream. All I wanted was a little piece of life, to be married, to have children. I thought the nightmares, the visions, the demons would go away if there was enough love to put them down. I was trying my damnedest to lead a conventional life, for that was how I was brought up, and it was what my husband wanted of me. But one can't build little white picket fences to keep nightmares out. The surface cracked when I was about twenty-eight. I had a psychotic break and tried to kill myself.

And you began to write after the nervous breakdown?

It isn't quite as simple as all that. I said to my doctor at the beginning, "I'm no good; I can't do anything; I'm dumb." He suggested I try educating myself by listening to Boston's educational TV station. He said I had a perfectly good mind. As a matter of fact, after he gave me a Rorschach test, he said I had creative talent that I wasn't using. I protested, but I followed his suggestion. One night I saw I. A. Richards on educational television reading a sonnet and explaining its form. I thought to myself, "I could do that, maybe; I could try." So I

---

*In this interview, Sexton repeats and expands upon some of her recollections of Robert Lowell's poetry workshop and her friendship with Sylvia Plath which had previously been published in "Classroom at Boston University" and "The Bar Fly Ought to Sing," both included in this volume.—ED.

sat down and wrote a sonnet. The next day I wrote another one, and so forth. My doctor encouraged me to write more. "Don't kill yourself," he said. "Your poems might mean something to someone else someday." That gave me a feeling of purpose, a little cause, something to *do* with my life, no matter how rotten I was.

Hadn't you written limericks before that?

I did write some light verse—for birthdays, for anniversaries, sometimes thank-you notes for weekends. Long before, I wrote some serious stuff in high school; however, I hadn't been exposed to any of the major poets, not even the minor ones. No one taught poetry at that school. I read nothing but Sara Teasdale. I might have read other poets but my mother said as I graduated from high school that I had plagiarized Sara Teasdale. Something about that statement of hers . . . I had been writing a poem a day for three months, but when she said that, I stopped.

Didn't anyone encourage you?

It wouldn't have mattered. My mother was top billing in our house.

In the beginning, what was the relationship between your poetry and your therapy?

Sometimes, my doctors tell me that I understand something in a poem that I haven't integrated into my life. In fact, I may be concealing it from myself, while I was revealing it to the readers. The poetry is often more advanced, in terms of my unconscious, than I am. Poetry, after all, milks the unconscious. The unconscious is there to feed it little images, little symbols, the answers, the insights I know not of. In therapy, one seeks to hide sometimes. I'll give you a rather intimate example of this. About three or four years ago my analyst asked me what I thought of my parents having intercourse when I was young. I couldn't talk. I knew there was suddenly a poem there, and I selfishly guarded it from him. Two days later, I had a poem, entitled, "In the Beach House," which describes overhearing the primal scene. In it I say, "Inside my prison of pine and bedspring, / over my window sill, under my knob, / it is plain that they are at / the royal strapping." The point of this little story is the image, "the royal strapping." My analyst was quite impressed with that image and so was I, although I don't remember going any further with it then. About three weeks ago, he said to me, "Were you ever beaten as a child?" I told him that I had been, when I was about nine. I had torn up a five-dollar bill that my father gave to my sister; my father took me into his bedroom, laid me down on his bed, pulled off my pants and beat me with a riding crop. As I related this to my doctor, he said, "See, that was quite a royal strapping," thus revealing to me, by way of my own image, the intensity of that moment, the sexuality of that beating, the little masochistic seizure—it's so classic, it's almost corny. Perhaps it's too intimate an example, but then both poetry and therapy are intimate.

Are your poems still closely connected to your therapy as in the past?

No. The subject of therapy was an early theme—the process itself as in "Said the Poet to the Analyst," the people of my past, admitting what my parents were really like, the whole Gothic New England story. I've had about eight doctors, but only two that count. I've written a poem for each of the two— "You, Doctor Martin" and "Cripples and Other Stories." And that will do. Those poems are about the two men as well as the strange process. One can say that my new poems, the love poems, come about as a result of new attitudes, an awareness of the possibly good as well as the possibly rotten. Inherent in the process is a rebirth of a sense of self, each time stripping away a dead self.

Some critics admire your ability to write about the terror of childhood guilts, parental deaths, breakdowns, suicides. Do you feel that writing about the dark parts of the human psyche takes a special act of courage?

Of course, but I'm tired of explaining it. It seems to be self-evident. There are warnings all along the way. "Go—children—slow." "It's dangerous in there." The appalling horror that awaits you in the answer.

People speak of you as a primitive. Was it so natural for you to dig so deeply into the painful experiences of your life?

There was a part of me that was horrified, but the gutsy part of me drove on. Still, part of me was appalled by what I was doing. On the one hand I was digging up shit, with the other hand, I was covering it with sand. Nevertheless, I went on ahead. I didn't know any better. Sometimes, I felt like a reporter researching himself. Yes, it took a certain courage, but as a writer one has to take the chance on being a fool . . . yes, to be a fool, that perhaps requires the greatest courage.

Once you began writing, did you attend any formal classes to bone up on technique?

After I'd been writing about three months, I dared to go into the poetry class at the Boston Center for Adult Education taught by John Holmes. I started in the middle of the term, very shy, writing very bad poems, solemnly handing them in for the eighteen others in the class to hear. The most important aspect of that class was that I felt I belonged somewhere. When I first got sick and became a displaced person, I thought I was quite alone, but when I went into the mental hospital, I found I wasn't, that there were other people like me. It made me feel better—more real, sane. I felt, "These are my people." Well, at the John Holmes class that I attended for two years, I found I belonged to the poets, that I was *real* there, and I had another, "These are my people." I met Maxine Kumin, the poet and novelist, at that class. She is my closest friend. She is part superego, part sister, as well as pal of my desk. It's strange because we're quite different. She is reserved, while I tend to be flamboyant. She is an intellectual, and I seem to be a primitive. That is true about our poetry as well.

You once told me, "I call Maxine Kumin every other line." Is that a slight exaggeration?

Yes. But often, I call her draft by draft. However, a lot of poems I did without her. The year I was writing my first book, I didn't know her well enough to call that often. Later, when she didn't approve of such poems as "Flee on Your Donkey"—that one took four years to complete—I was on my own. Yet once, she totally saved a poem, "Cripples and Other Stories."

In the early days, how did your relatives react to the jangling of family skeletons?

I tried not to show my relatives any of the poems. I do know that my mother snuck into my desk one time and read "The Double Image" before it was printed. She told me just before she died that she liked the poem, and that saved me from some added guilt. My husband liked that poem, too. Ordinarily, if I show him a poem, something I try not to do, he says, "I don't think that's too hotsy-totsy," which puts me off. I try not to do it too often. My in-laws don't approve of the poems at all. My children do—with a little pain, they do.

In your poems, several family skeletons come out of the camphor balls—your father's alcoholic tendencies, your mother's inability to deal with your suicide attempt, your great-aunt in a strait jacket. Is there any rule you follow as to which skeletons you reveal and which you don't?

I don't reveal skeletons that would hurt anyone. They may hurt the dead, but the dead belong to me. Only once in a while do they talk back. For instance, I don't write about my husband or his family, although there are some amazing stories there.

How about Holmes or the poets in your class, what did they say?

During the years of that class, John Holmes saw me as something evil and warned Maxine to stay away from me. He told me I shouldn't write such personal poems about the madhouse. He said, "That isn't a fit subject for poetry." I knew no one who thought it was; even my doctor clammed up at that time. I was on my own. I tried to mind them. I tried to write the way the others, especially Maxine, wrote, but it didn't work. I always ended up sounding like myself.

You have said, "If anything influenced me, it was W. D. Snodgrass's "Heart's Needle." Would you comment on that?

If he had the courage, then I had the courage. That poem about losing his daughter brought me to face some of the facts about my own life. I had lost a daughter, lost her because I was too sick to keep her. After I read the poem, "Heart's Needle," I ran up to my mother-in-law's house and brought my daughter home. That's what a poem should do—move people to action. True, I didn't keep my daughter at the time—I wasn't ready. But I was beginning to be ready. I wrote a disguised poem about it, "Unknown Girl in the Maternity Ward." The pain of the loss . . .

Did you ever meet Snodgrass?

Yes. I'd read "Heart's Needle" in *The New Poets of England and America.* I'd written about three quarters of *To Bedlam and Part Way Back* at the time, and I made a pilgrimage to Antioch Writer's Conference to meet and to learn from Snodgrass. He was a surprising person, surprisingly humble. He encouraged me, he liked what I was doing. He was the first established poet to like my work, and so I was driven to write harder and to allow myself, to dare myself to tell the whole story. He also suggested that I study with Robert Lowell. So I sent Mr. Lowell some of my poems and asked if he would take me into the class. By then I'd had poems published in the *New Yorker* and around a bit. At any rate, the poems seemed good enough for Lowell and I joined the class.

Which poems did you submit to Lowell?

As far as I can remember, the poems about madness—"You, Doctor Martin," "Music Swims Back to Me" . . . about ten or fifteen poems from the book.

Was this before or after Lowell published Life Studies?

Before. I sent him the poems in the summer; the following spring *Life Studies* came out. Everyone says I was influenced by Robert Lowell's revelation of madness in that book, but I was writing *To Bedlam and Part Way Back,* the story of my madness, before *Life Studies* was published. I showed my poems to Mr. Lowell as he was working on his book. Perhaps I even influenced him. I have never asked him. But stranger things have happened.

And when was your first book, To Bedlam and Part Way Back, *published?*

It was accepted that January; it wasn't published for a year and a half after that, I think.

Where was Lowell teaching then?

The class met at Boston University on Tuesdays from two to four in a dismal room. It consisted of some twenty students. Seventeen graduates, two other housewives who were graduates or something, and a boy who had snuck over from MIT. I was the only one in that room who hadn't read *Lord Weary's Castle.*

And Lowell, how did he strike you?

He was formal in a rather awkward New England sense. His voice was soft and slow as he read the students' poems. At first I felt the impatient desire to interrupt his slow, line-by-line readings. He would read the first line, stop, and then discuss it at length. I wanted to go through the whole poem quickly and then go back. I couldn't see any merit in dragging through it until you almost hated the damned thing, even your own poems, especially your own. At that point, I wrote to Snodgrass about my impatience, and his reply went this way, "Frankly, I used to nod my head at his every statement, and he taught me more than a whole gang of scholars could." So I kept my mouth shut, and Snodgrass was right. Robert Lowell's method of teaching is intuitive and open. After he had read a student's poem, he would read another evoked by it. Comparison was often painful. He worked with a cold chisel, with no more mercy than a dentist. He got out the decay, but if he was never kind to the poem, he was kind to the poet.

Did you consult Robert Lowell on your manuscript of To Bedlam and Part Way Back *before you submitted it to a publisher?*

Yes. I gave him a manuscript to see if he thought it was a book. He was enthusiastic on the whole, but suggested that I throw out about half of it and write another fifteen or so poems that were better. He pointed out the weak ones, and I nodded and took them out. It sounds simple to say that I merely, as he once said, "jumped the hurdles that he had put up," but it makes a difference who puts up the hurdles. He defined the course, and acted as though, good race horse that I was, I would just naturally run it.

Ultimately, what can a teacher give a writer in a creative-writing class?

Courage, of course. That's the most important ingredient. Then, in a rather plain way, Lowell helped me to distrust the easy musical phrase and to look for the frankness of ordinary speech. Lowell is never impressed with a display of images or sounds—those things that a poet is born with anyhow. If you have enough natural imagery, he can show you how to chain it in. He didn't teach me what to put into a poem, but what to leave out. What he taught me was taste—perhaps that's the only thing a poet can be taught.

Sylvia Plath was a member of Lowell's class also, wasn't she?

Yes. She and George Starbuck heard that I was auditing Lowell's class. They kind of joined me there for the second term. After the class, we would pile in the front seat of my old Ford and I would drive quickly through the traffic to the Ritz. I would always park illegally in a LOADING ONLY ZONE, telling them gaily, "It's okay, we're only going to get loaded." Off we'd go, each on George's arm, into the Ritz to drink three or four martinis. George even has a line about this in his first book of poems, *Bone Thoughts*. After the Ritz, we would spend our last pennies at the Waldorf Cafeteria—a dinner for seventy cents—George was in no hurry. He was separated from his wife; Sylvia's Ted [Hughes] was busy with his own work, and I had to stay in the city for a seven P.M. appointment with my psychiatrist . . . a funny three.

In Sylvia Plath's last book, written just before her suicide, she was submerged by the theme of death, as you are in your book, Live or Die. *Did you ever get around to talking about death or your suicides at the Ritz?*

Often, very often. Sylvia and I would talk at length about our first suicide, in detail and in depth—between the free potato chips. Suicide is, after all, the opposite of the poem. Sylvia and I often talked opposites. We talked death with burned-up intensity, both of us drawn to it like moths to an electric light bulb, sucking on it. She told the story of her first suicide in sweet and loving detail, and her description in *The Bell Jar* is just that same story. It is a wonder we didn't depress George with our egocentricity; instead, I think, we three were stimulated by it—even George—as if death made each of us a little more real at the moment.

In a BBC interview, Sylvia Plath said, "I've been very excited by what I feel is the new breakthrough that came with, say, Robert Lowell's Life Studies. . . . *This intense breakthrough into very serious, very personal emotional experience, which I feel has been partly taboo . . . I think particularly of the poetess Anne Sexton, who writes also about her experiences as a mother; as a mother who's had a nervous breakdown, as an extremely emotional and feeling young woman. And her poems are wonderfully craftsmanlike poems, and yet they have a kind of emotional psychological depth, which I think is something perhaps quite new and exciting." Do you agree that you influenced her?*

Maybe. I did give her a sort of daring, but that's all she should have said. I remember writing to Sylvia in England after her first book, *The Colossus*, came out and saying something like, "If you're not careful, Sylvia, you will out-Roethke Roethke." She replied that I had guessed accurately. But maybe she buried her so-called influences deeper than that, deeper than any one of us would think to look, and if she did, I say, "Good luck to her!" Her poems do their own work. I don't need to sniff them for distant relatives: I'm against it.

Did Sylvia Plath influence your writing?

Her first book didn't interest me at all. I was doing my own thing. But after her death, with the appearance of *Ariel*, I think I was influenced and I don't mind saying it. In a special sort of way, it was daring again. She had dared to do something quite different. She had dared to write hate poems, the one thing I had never dared to write. I'd always been afraid, even in my life, to express anger. I think the poem, "Cripples and Other Stories," is evidence of a hate poem somehow, though no one could ever write a poem to compare to her "Daddy." There was a kind of insolence in them, saying,

"Daddy, you bastard, I'm through." I think the poem, "The Addict," has some of her speech rhythms in it. She had very open speech rhythms, something that I didn't always have.

You have said, "I think the second book lacks some of the impact and honesty of the first, which I wrote when I was so raw that I didn't know any better." Would you describe your development from the second book to the third and from your third to the fourth?

Well, in the first book, I was giving the experience of madness; in the second book, the causes of madness; and in the third book, finally, I find that I was deciding whether to live or to die. In the third I was daring to be a fool again—raw, "uncooked," as Lowell calls it, with a little camouflage. In the fourth book, I not only have lived, come on to the scene, but loved, that sometime miracle.

What would you say about the technical development from book to book?

In *Bedlam,* I used very tight form in most cases, feeling that I could express myself better. I take a kind of pleasure, even now, but more especially in *Bedlam,* in forming a stanza, a verse, making it an entity, and then coming to a little conclusion at the end of it, of a little shock, a little double rhyme shock. In my second book, *All My Pretty Ones,* I loosened up and in the last section didn't use any form at all. I found myself to be surprisingly free without the form which had worked as a kind of superego for me. The third book I used less form. In *Love Poems,* I had one long poem, eighteen sections, that is in form and I enjoyed doing it in that way. With the exception of that and a few other poems, all of the book is in free verse, and I feel at this point comfortable to use either, depending on what the poem requires.

Is there any particular subject which you'd rather deal with in form than in free verse?

Probably madness. I've noticed that Robert Lowell felt freer to write about madness in free verse, whereas it was the opposite for me. Only after I had set up large structures that were almost impossible to deal with did I think I was free to allow myself to express what had really happened. However in *Live or Die,* I wrote "Flee on Your Donkey" without that form and found that I could do it just as easily in free verse. That's perhaps something to do with my development as a human being and understanding of myself, besides as a poet.

In Live or Die, *the whole book has a marvelous structured tension— simply by the sequence of the poems which pits the wish to live against the death instinct. Did you plan the book this way? Lois Ames speaks of you as wishing to write more "live" poems because the "die" poems outnumbered them.*

I didn't plan the book any way. In January of 1962, I started collecting new poems the way you do when a book is over. I didn't know where they would go or that they would go anywhere, even into a book. Then at some point, as I was collecting these poems, I was rereading *Henderson the Rain King* by Saul Bellow. I had met Saul Bellow at a cocktail party about a year before and I had been carrying *Henderson the Rain King* around in my suitcase everywhere I traveled. Suddenly there I was meeting Saul Bellow, and I was overenthusiastic. I said, "Oh, oh, you're Saul Bellow, I've wanted to meet you," and he ran from the room. Very afraid. I was quite ashamed of my exuberance and then sometime, a year later, reading *Henderson the Rain King* over again, at three in the morning, I wrote Saul Bellow a fan letter about Henderson, saying that he was a monster of despair, that I understood his position because Henderson was the one who had ruined life, who had blown up the frogs, made a mess out of everything. I drove to the mail box then and there! The next morning I wrote him a letter of apology.

Saul Bellow wrote me back on the back of a manuscript. He said to me, "Luckily, I have a message to you from the book I am writing [which was *Herzog*]. I have both your letters—the good one which was written that night at three A.M. and then the contrite one, the next day. One's best things are always followed by apoplectic, apologetic seizure. Monster of despair could be *Henderson*'s subtitle." The message that he had encircled went this way, "With one long breath, caught and held in his chest, he fought his sadness over his solitary life. Don't cry, you idiot! Live or die, but don't poison everything." And in circling that and in sending it to me, Saul Bellow had given me a message about my whole life. That I didn't want to poison the world, that I didn't want to be the killer; I wanted to be the one who gave birth, who encouraged things to grow and to flower, not the poisoner. So I stuck that message up over my desk and it was a kind of hidden message. You don't know what these messages mean to you, yet you stick them up over your desk or remember them or write them down and put them in your wallet. One day I was reading a quote from Rimbaud that said, "Anne, Anne, flee on your donkey," and I typed it out because it had my name in it and because I wanted to flee. I put it in my wallet, went to see my doctor, and at that point was committed to a hospital for about the seventh or eighth time. In the hospital, I started to write the poem, "Flee on Your Donkey," as though the message had come to me at just the right moment. Well, this was true with Bellow's quote from his book. I kept it over my desk and when I went to Europe, I pasted it in the front of my manuscript. I kept it there as a quotation with which to preface my book. It must have just hit me one day that *Live or Die* was a damn good title for the book I was working on. And that's what it was all about, what all those poems were about. You say there's a tension there and a structure, but it was an unconscious tension and an unconscious structure that I didn't know was going on when I was doing it.

Once you knew the title of the book, did you count up the "live" poems and count up the "die" poems and then write any more poems because of an imbalance?

No, no, that's far too rigid. You can't write a poem because of an imbalance. After that I wrote "Little Girl, My Stringbean, My Lovely Woman." Then I wrote a play, then "A Little Uncomplicated Hymn" and other poems. Some were negative and some were positive. At this time I knew that I was trying to get a book together. I had more than enough for a book, but I knew I hadn't written out the live or die question. I hadn't written the poem "Live." This was bothering me because it wasn't coming to me. Instead of that, "Cripples and Other Stories" and "The Addict" were appearing, and I knew that I wasn't finishing the book, that I hadn't come to the cycle, I hadn't given a reason. There's nothing I could do about this and then suddenly, our dog was pregnant. I was supposed to kill all the puppies when they came; instead, I let them live and I realized that if I let *them* live, that I could let *me* live, too, that after all I wasn't a killer, that the poison just didn't take.

Although you received a European traveling fellowship from the American Academy of Arts and Letters, there are, to date, very few poems published about your European experience. Why?

First of all poems aren't postcards to send home. Secondly I went to Europe with a purpose as well as with a grant. My great-aunt, who was really my best childhood friend, had sent letters home from Europe the three years that she lived there. I had written about this in a poem called "Some Foreign Letters." I had her letters with me as I left for Europe and I was going to walk her walks, and go to her places, live her life over again, and write letters back to her. The two poems that I did write about Europe mention the letters. In "Crossing the Atlantic," I mention that I have read my grandmother's letters, and my mother's letters. I had swallowed their words like Dickens, thinking of Dickens's journals in America. The second poem, "Walking in Paris," was written about my great-aunt, how she used to walk fourteen or fifteen miles a day in Paris, and I call her Nana. Some critics have thought I meant

Zola's Nana, but I didn't any more than I meant the Nana in Peter Pan. However, the letters were stolen from my car in Belgium. When I lost the letters in Brussels, that was the end of that kind of poem that I had gone over there to write.

You were to go abroad for a year, but you only stayed two months. Do you want to comment on that?

Two and a half months. I got sick over there; I lost my sense of self. I had, as my psychiatrist said, "a leaky ego" and I had to come home. I was in the hospital for a while and then I returned to my normal life. I had to come home because I need my husband and my therapist and my children to tell me who I am. I remember, I was talking with Elizabeth Hardwick on the phone and saying, "Oh, I feel so guilty. I couldn't get along without my husband. It's a terrible thing, really, a modern woman should be able to do it." Although I may be misquoting her, I may have remembered it the way I needed to hear it, she said to me, "If I were in Paris without my husband, I'd hide in a hotel room all day." And I said, "Well, think of Mary McCarthy." And Elizabeth Hardwick said, "Mary McCarthy, she's never been without a man for a day in her life."

From 1964 to 1965, you held a Ford Foundation Grant in playwriting and worked at Boston's Charles Street Playhouse. How did you feel writing something that had to be staged?

I felt great! I used to pace up and down the living room shouting out the lines, and what do they call it . . . for walking around the stage . . . *blocking* out the play as I would go along.

*Was the play [*Mercy Street*] ever performed?**

---

*For details on a later professional production of this play, see Sexton's interview with Lois Ames, reprinted in this volume, pp. 119–129.—Ed.

There were little working performances at the Charles Playhouse when we had time. It was pretty busy there. Now and then they would play out a scene for me, and then I would rewrite it and send it in to the director special delivery. He would call me up the next morning and say, "It's not right," and then I would work on it again, send it to him that evening, and then the next morning, he'd call, and so on it went. I found that I had one whole character in the play who was unnecessary because, as they acted it, the director had that person be quiet and say nothing. I realized that that dialogue was totally unnecessary, so I cut out that character.

Did you find that the themes in your poetry overlapped into your play? Was your play an extension of your poetry?

Yes. Completely. The play was about a girl shuffling between her psychiatrist and a priest. It was the priest I cut out, realizing that she really wasn't having a dialogue with him at all. The play was about all the subjects that my poems are about— my mother, my great-aunt, my father, and the girl who wants to kill herself. A little bit about her husband, but not much. The play is really a morality play. The second act takes place after death.

Many of your poems are dramatic narratives. Because you're accustomed to handling a plot, was it easy for you to switch from verse to scene writing?

I don't see the difference. In both cases, the character is confronting himself and his destiny. I didn't know I was writing scenes; I thought I was writing about people. In another context—helping Maxine Kumin with her novel—I gave her a bit of advice. I told her, "Fuck structure and grab your characters by the time balls." Each one of us sits in our time; we're born, live and die. She was thinking this and that and I was telling her to get inside her characters' lives—which she finally did.

What were your feelings when you received the Pulitzer Prize for Poetry for Live or Die *in 1967?*

Of course, I was delighted. It had been a bad time for me. I had a broken hip and I was just starting to get well, still crippled, but functioning a little bit. After I received the prize, it gave me added incentive to write more. In the months following, I managed to write a poem, "Eighteen Days Without You," in fourteen days—an eighteen-section poem. I was inspired by the recognition that the Pulitzer gave me, even though I was aware that it didn't mean all that much. After all, they have to give a Pulitzer Prize every year and I was just one in a long line.

Do you write a spate of poems at one time or are you disciplined by a writing schedule?

Well, I'm very dissatisfied with the amount I write. My first book—although it took three years to complete—was really written in one year. Sometimes ten poems were written in two weeks. When I was going at that rate, I found that I could really work well. Now I tend to become dissatisfied with the fact that I write poems so slowly, that they come to me so slowly. When they come, I write them; when they don't come, I don't. There's certainly no disciplined writing schedule, except for the fact that when a poem comes a person must be disciplined and ready flexing his muscles. That is they burst forth and you must put everything else aside. Ideally it doesn't matter what it is, unless your husband has double pneumonia or the child breaks his leg. Otherwise, you don't tear yourself away from the typewriter until you must sleep.

Do the responsibilities of wife and mother interfere with your writing?

Well, when my children were younger, they interfered all the time. It was just my stubbornness that let me get through with it at all, because here were these young children saying, "Momma, Momma," and there I was getting the images, structuring the poem. Now my children are older and creep around the house saying, "Shh, Mother is writing a poem." But then again, as I was writing the poem, "Eighteen Days Without You"—the last poem in *Love Poems*—my husband said to me, "I can't stand it any longer, you haven't been with me for days." That poem originally was "Twenty-one Days Without You" and it became "Eighteen Days" because he had cut into the inspiration; he demanded my presence back again, into his life, and I couldn't take that much from him.

When writing, what part of the poem is the prickliest part?

Punctuation, sometimes. The punctuating can change the whole meaning, and my life is full of little dots and dashes. Therefore, I have to let the editors help me punctuate. And, probably the rhythm. It's the thing I have to work hardest to get in the beginning—the feeling, the voice of the poem, and how it will come across, how it will feel to the reader, how it feels to me as it comes out. Images are probably the most important part of the poem. First of all, you want to tell a story, but images are what are going to shore it up and get to the heart of the matter—but I don't have to work too hard for the images—they have to come—if they're not coming, I'm not even writing a poem, it's pointless. So I work hardest to get the rhythm, because each poem should have its own rhythm, its own structure. Each poem has its own life, each one is different.

How do you decide a length of line? Does it have something to do with the way it looks on a page as well as how many beats there are to a line?

How it looks on a page. I don't give a damn about the beats in a line, unless I want them and need them. These are just tricks that you use when you need them. It's a very simple thing to write with rhyme and with rhythmic beat—those things anyone can do nowadays; everyone is quite accomplished at that. The point, the hard thing, is to get the true voice of the poem, to make each poem an individual thing, give it the stamp of your own voice, and at the same time to make it singular.

Do you ever find yourself saying, "Oh, yes, I've explored that in another poem," and discarding a poem?

No, because I might want to explore it in a new way . . . I might have a new realization, a new truth about it. Recently I noticed in "Flee on Your Donkey" that I had used some of the same facts in *To Bedlam and Part Way Back,* but I hadn't realized them in their total ugliness. I'd hidden from them. This time was really raw and really ugly and it was all involved with my own madness. It was all like a great involuted web, and I presented it the way it really was.

Do you revise a great deal?

Constantly.

Do you have any ritual which gets you set for writing?

I might, if I felt the poem come on, put on a certain record, sometimes the "Bachianas Brasileiras" by Villa-Lobos. I wrote to that for about three or four years. It's my magic tune.

Is there any time of day, any particular mood that is better for writing?

No. Those moments before a poem comes, when the heightened awareness comes over you and you realize a poem is buried there somewhere, you prepare yourself. I run around, you know, kind of skipping around the house, marvelous elation. It's as though I could fly, almost, and I get very tense before I've told the truth—hard. Then I sit down at the desk and get going with it.

What is the quality of feeling when you're writing?

Well, it's a beautiful feeling, even if it's hard work. When I'm writing, I know I'm doing the thing I was born to do.

Do you have any standard by which you judge whether to let an image remain in a poem, or be cut?

It's done with my unconscious. May it do me no ill.

You've said, "When I'm working away on a poem, I hunt for the truth. . . . It might be a poetic truth, and not just a factual one." Can you comment on that?

Many of my poems are true, line by line, altering a few facts to get the story at its heart. In "The Double Image," the poem about my mother's death from cancer and the loss of my daughter, I don't mention that I had another child. Each poem has its own truth. Furthermore, in that poem, I only say that I was hospitalized twice, when in fact, I was hospitalized five times in that span of time. But then, poetic truth is not necessarily autobiographical. It is truth that goes beyond the immediate self, another life. I don't adhere to literal facts all the time; I make them up whenever needed. Concrete examples give a verisimilitude. I want the reader to feel, "Yes, yes, that's the way it is." I want them to feel as if they were touching me. I would alter any word, attitude, image or persona for the sake of a poem. As Yeats said, "I have lived many lives, I have been a slave and a prince. Many a beloved has sat upon my knee, and I have sat upon the knee of many a beloved. Everything that has been shall be again."

There Yeats is talking about reincarnation.

So am I. It's a little mad, but I believe I am many people. When I am writing a poem, I feel I am the person who should have written it. Many times I assume these guises; I attack it the way a novelist might. Sometimes I become someone else and when I do, I believe, even in moments when I'm not writing the poem, that I am that person. When I wrote about the farmer's wife, I lived in my mind in Illinois; when I had the illegitimate child, I nursed it—in my mind—and gave it back and traded life. When I gave my lover back to his wife, in my mind, I grieved and saw how ethereal and unnecessary I had been. When I was Christ, I felt like Christ. My arms hurt, I desperately wanted to pull them in off the Cross. When I was taken down off the Cross, and buried alive, I sought solutions; I hoped they were Christian solutions.

What prompted you to write "In the Deep Museum," which recounts what Christ could have felt if he were still alive in the tomb? What led you to even deal with such a subject?

I'm not sure. I think it was an unconscious thing. I think I had a kind of feeling Christ was speaking to me and telling me to write that story . . . the story he hadn't written. I thought to myself, this would be the most awful death. The Cross, the Crucifixion which I so deeply believe in has almost become trite, and that there was a more humble death that he might have had to seek for love's sake, because his love was the greatest thing about him—not his death.

Are you a believing nonbeliever? Your poems, such as "The Division of Parts" and "With Mercy for the Greedy," suggest you would like to believe, indeed struggle to believe, but can't.

Yes. I fight my own impulse. There is a hard-core part of me that believes, and there's this little critic in me that believes nothing. Some people think I'm a lapsed Catholic.

What was your early religious training?

Half-assed Protestant. My Nana came from a Protestant background with a very stern patriarchal father who had twelve children. He often traveled in Europe, and when he came back and brought nude statues into his house, the minister came to call and said, "You can't come to church if you keep these nude statues." So he said, "All right, I'll never come again." Every Sunday morning he read the Bible to his twelve children for two hours, and they had to sit up straight and perfect. He never went to church again.

Where do you get the "juice" for your religious poetry?

I found when I was bringing up my children, that I could answer questions about sex easily. But I had a very hard time with the questions about God and death. It isn't resolved in my mind to this day.

Are you saying then that questions from your children are what prompted you to think about these poems—that doesn't sound quite right.

It isn't. I have visions—sometimes ritualized visions—that come to me of God, or of Christ, or of the Saints, and I feel that I can touch them almost . . . that they are part of me. It's the same "Everything that has been shall be again." It's reincarnation, speaking with another voice . . . or else with the Devil. If you want to know the truth, the leaves talk to me every June.

How long do your visions last? What are they like?

That's impossible to describe. They could last for six months, six minutes or six hours. I feel very much in touch with things after I've had a vision. It's somewhat like the beginning of writing a poem; the whole world is very sharp and well-defined, and I'm intensely alive, like I've been shot full of electric volts.

Do you try to communicate this to other people when you feel it?

Only through the poems, no other way. I refuse to talk about it, which is why I'm having a hard time now.

Is there any real difference between a religious vision and a vision when you're mad?

Sometimes, when you're mad, the vision—I don't call them visions really—when you're mad, they're silly and out of place, whereas if it's a so-called mystical experience, you've put everything in its proper place. I've never talked about my religious experiences with anyone, not a psychiatrist, not a friend, not a priest, not anyone. I've kept it very much to myself—and I find this very difficult, and I'd just as soon leave it, if you please.

A poem like "The Division of Parts" has direct reference to your mother's dying. Did those excruciating experiences of watching someone close to you disintegrate from cancer force you to confront your own belief in God or religion?

Yes, I think so. The dying are slowly being rocked away from us and wrapped up into death, that eternal place. And one looks for answers and is faced with demons and visions. Then one comes up with God. I don't mean the ritualized Protestant God, who is such a goody-goody . . . but the martyred saints, the crucified man . . .

Are you saying that when confronted with the ultimate question, death, that your comfort comes, even though watered-down, from the myths and fables of religion?

No myth or fable ever gave me any solace, but my own inner contact with the heroes of the fables, as you put it, my very closeness to Christ. In one poem about the Virgin Mary, "For the Year of the Insane," I believed that I was talking to Mary, that her lips were upon my lips; it's almost physical . . . as in many of my poems. I become that person.

But is it the fact in your life of someone you know dying that forces you into a vision?

No, I think it's my own madness.

Are you more lucid, in the sense of understanding life, when you are mad?

Yes.

Why do you think that's so?

Pure gift.

I asked you, are you a believing disbeliever. When something happens like a death, are you pushed over the brink of disbelieving into believing?

For a while, but it can happen without a death. There are little deaths in life, too—in your own life—and at that point, sometimes you are in touch with strange things, otherworldly things.

You have received a great deal of fan mail from Jesuits and other clergy. Do any of them interpret what you write as blasphemy?

No. They find my work very religious, and take my books on retreats, and teach my poems in classes.

Why do you feel that most of your critics ignore this strain of religious experience in your poetry?

I think they tackle the obvious things, without delving deeper. They are more shocked by the other, whereas I think in time to come people will be more shocked by my mystical poetry than by my so-called confessional poetry.

Perhaps your critics, in time to come, will associate the suffering in your confessional poetry with the kind of sufferers you take on in your religious poetry.

You've summed it up perfectly. Thank you for saying that. That ragged Christ, that sufferer, performed the greatest act of confession, and I mean with his body. And I try to do that with words.

Many of your poems deal with memories of suffering. Very few of them deal with memories that are happy ones. Why do you feel driven to write more about pain?

That's not true about my last book, which deals with joy. I think I've dealt with unhappy themes because I've lived them. If I haven't lived them, I've invented them.

But surely there were also happy moments, joyous, euphoric moments in those times as well.

Pain engraves a deeper memory.

Are there any poems you wouldn't read in public?

No. As a matter of fact, I sing "Cripples and Other Stories" with my combo to a Nashville rhythm.

What is your combo?

It's called "Her Kind"—after one of my poems. One of my students started putting my poems to music—he's a guitarist and then we got an organist, a flutist and a drummer. We call our music "Chamber Rock." We've been working on it and giving performances for about a year. It opens up my poems in a new way, by involving them in the sound of rock music, letting my words open up to sound that can be actually heard, giving a new dimension. And it's quite exciting for me to hear them that way.

Do you enjoy giving a reading?

It takes three weeks out of your life. A week before it happens, the nervousness begins and it builds up to the night of the reading, when the poet in you changes into a performer. Readings take so much out of you, because they are a reliving of the experience, that is, they are happening all over again. I am an actress in my own autobiographical play. Then there is the love. . . . When there is a coupling of the audience and myself, when they are really with me, and the Muse is with me, I'm not coming alone.

Can you ever imagine America as a place where thousands of fans flock to a stadium to hear a poet, as they do in Russia?

Someday, perhaps. But our poets seem to be losing touch. People flock to Bob Dylan, Janis Joplin, the Beatles—these are the popular poets of the English-speaking world. But I don't worry about popularity; I'm too busy.

At first your poetry was a therapeutic device. Why do you write now?

I write because I'm driven to—it's my bag. Though after every book, I think there'll never be another one. That's the end of that. Good-bye, good-bye.

And what advice would you give to a young poet?

Be careful who your critics are. Be specific. Tell almost the whole story. Put your ear close down to your soul and listen hard.

Louis Simpson criticised your poetry saying, "A poem titled 'Menstruation at Forty' was the straw that broke this camel's back." Is it only male critics who balk at your use of the biological facts of womanhood?

I haven't added up all the critics and put them on different teams. I haven't noticed the gender of the critic especially. I talk of the life-death cycle of the body. Well, women tell time by the body. They are like clocks. They are always fastened to the earth, listening for its small animal noises. Sexuality is one of the most normal parts of life. True, I get a little uptight when Norman Mailer writes that he screws a woman anally. I like Allen Ginsberg very much and when he writes about the ugly vagina, I feel awful. That kind of thing doesn't appeal to me. So I have my limitations, too. Homosexuality is all right with me. Sappho was beautiful. But when someone hates another person's body and somehow violates it—that's the kind of thing I mind.

What do you feel is the purpose of poetry?

As Kafka said about prose, "A book should serve as the axe for the frozen sea within us." And that's what I want from a poem. A poem should serve as the axe for the frozen sea within us.

How would you apply the Kafka quote to your new book, Love Poems?

Well, have you ever seen a sixteen-year-old fall in love? The axe for the frozen sea becomes imbedded in her. Or have you ever seen a woman get to be forty and never have any love in her life? What happens to her when she falls in love? The axe for the frozen sea.

Some people wonder how you can write about yourself, completely ignoring the great issues of the times, like the Vietnam War or the civil rights crisis.

People have to find out who they are before they can confront national issues. The fact that I seldom write about public issues in no way reflects my personal opinion. I am a pacifist. I sign petitions, etc. However, I am not a polemicist. "The Fire Bombers"—that's a new poem—is about wanton destruction, not about Vietnam, specifically; when Robert Kennedy was killed, I wrote about an assassin. I write about human emotions; I write about interior events, not historical ones. In one of my love poems, I say that my lover is unloading bodies from Vietnam. If that poem is read in a hundred years, people will have to look up the war in Vietnam. They will have mixed it up with the Korean or God knows what else. One hopes it will be history very soon. Of course, I may change. I could use the specifics of the war for a backdrop against which to reveal experience, and it would be just as valid as the details I am known by. As for the civil rights issue, I mentioned that casually in a poem, but I don't go into it. I think it's a major issue. I think many of my poems about the individual who is dispossessed, who must play slave, who cries "Freedom Now," "Power Now," are about the human experience of being black in this world. A black emotion can be a white emotion. It is a crisis for the individual as well as the nation. I think I've been writing black poems all along, wearing my white mask. I'm always the victim . . . but no longer!

With Brigitte Weeks

Although she only began writing poetry in 1957, Anne Sexton has become one of this country's major poets, establishing an intensely personal and candid voice with her first volume of poems, To Bedlam and Part Way Back, *published in 1960. No less intimate were her next two books,* All My Pretty Ones, *in 1962, and* Live or Die, *in 1966, the latter of which was awarded the Pulitzer Prize for poetry. Born and raised in the Boston area, Mrs. Sexton combines her writing career with being wife and mother in a residential suburb of the city.*

Have you always lived in New England?

Yes, I've been around here all my life—I grew up in Wellesley and Weston. My husband and I did live in Baltimore and San Francisco for a while, when he was in the Navy.

I was interested to read somewhere that you had never had a college education. Was that by choice, or by circumstance?

Well, that's often said about me, but it isn't quite true—I did go to college for a year, to Garland. It's a junior college. I studied mostly cooking, sewing, and childcare—things like that. Then I eloped.

You must have been fairly young.

Nineteen.

What is your husband's profession?

He's a wool salesman.

What is his attitude to your poetry?

Well, he's not really that interested. He does occasionally read my books when they're finished, but I don't think he really likes poetry very much. It's probably a very good thing for me. You need to be detached from your work sometimes.

What was your reaction to winning the Pulitzer Prize with Live or Die?

Of course, I was very excited, though I was surprised too. I thought both the other books were as good, and since they didn't win a Pulitzer, I thought no book of mine ever would.

Do you have a new book under way?

Yes, I just sent the manuscript to my publishers, so that now I'm in kind of a dead period. That always happens after completing a book. Your heart is still with it until you actually see the galleys, but when I hold the work in my hand it seems to have a kind of unity, especially if I like the look of it, and my publishers have always made nice-looking books for me.

Does the new book have a dominant theme?

It's called *Love Poems*, so the theme is obvious from that. It's hard for me to be objective about it yet. I'm too close to it and it's still like looking at it through magnified lenses. I wasn't really sure of the others but now it's more difficult since I have something to live up to. In the beginning I was just thrilled to have a book published. But I do think this is a happier book than the others. My poetry has tended to become more imagistic.

Does that make it more obscure?

No, I certainly hope not. In my early books there were always one or two poems that I thought people would not understand. I don't think there are any of those in the new book if that is important. The main thing is to communicate, so I want my poems to be immediately comprehensible. For me poems are verbal happenings. I start with a feeling—no more than that. Then you must open up, lay yourself open to all possibilities. The next stage, I think, is ordering it—for clarity and to make a meaningful impact. Of course, opening a poem up to all possibilities makes bad lines inevitable. That's why I go through so many drafts for one poem. I used to spend all my time writing poetry, but I don't write as much now. I think some of the sensation goes on in my head and never reaches paper.

Does anyone beside yourself play an active part in the selection process?

Not really—well, I do have a close friend who is a poet too and sometimes I read them to her in first draft. She has an understanding of the process because she writes poetry herself. I sometimes take her advice, especially if I'm unsure of myself. If I know that I'm right, I don't take any advice. I suppose all poets have a little critic in their heads. I do—but you have to turn off the little critic while you are beginning a poem so that it doesn't inhibit you. Then you have to turn it on again when you are revising and refining. That's a very important stage.

People are always fascinated with the mechanics of how writing happens. Do you work to any regular system?

Not really. Sometimes I get the feeling that there is a poem around. It's a kind of heightened awareness, like a shot of adrenaline. Sometimes nothing happens. But when I do start to write it is a very concentrated process. I don't stop—even the children know now that when Mommy's writing she mustn't be disturbed. Of course, that wasn't the case when they were small. I was often disturbed then!

Did being interrupted ever cause you to lose a poem, the way Coleridge forgot the end of "Kubla Khan" when someone came to the door?

I don't think so—perhaps. But if it was important it would come back in some form or other.

If the creation of a poem is a matter of sudden inspiration, apparently arbitrary, do you think that education and training are of little real aid to a writer or a poet?

No, I don't, definitely not. It's just like a runner getting into training or a fighter hitting a punching bag. You need to be in shape. You need the means, the equipment to be equal to the moment of inspiration when it comes. Otherwise, you can do nothing.

I notice that when you are speaking of your poetry the words truth, excitement, *and* magic *often recur—are they crucial?*

Yes, that and courage. You need courage to overcome the little inherent deceits in yourself and stamina to bring the truth alive in a poem. That is what I mean by *truth*—there is a lot of unconscious truth in a poem. In some ways, as you see me now, I am a lie. The crystal truth is in my poetry.

Do you learn about yourself from this truth revealed unconsciously in your poetry?

I think I could. Sometimes I don't know whether I want to. I suppose it's like willingness to remember a dream. You don't remember what you want to suppress.

Can you analyze the magic any more closely?

I can't, but then I'm not sure that I want to. Obviously it is *your* job to try to analyze, but in a way it is *mine* to try to hide. I don't really know what the magic is—as I said before it begins with a kind of heightened awareness.

Is it difficult to discipline this magic into poetic form?

No, I often work to a very rigid form, although not so often as when I began writing poetry. My conventions are my own, but if the magic is there I can work with almost any form. It often changes with each section of a poem.

Is the form dictated by the subject matter?

No, more by the look of the first line—the way it feels. At first I did not make my own forms. I used to copy other people's forms, like Edna St. Vincent Millay's, for example. Then one day I decided to formulate my own.

Birth, death, and love seem to have been the dominant themes in your poetry. Do you think they are crucial poetic themes?

Yes, I do. I often find that it is a test of a poet's ability to write an elegy on, say, the death of a parent. If a poet proves equal to such a demand then usually he has the magic.

If birth is a crucial theme of poetry, does that mean that men are denied a whole area of poetic expression?

No I don't think so. Women don't like it said, but I think men are just as capable as women of understanding the experience of birth—for instance, they can bear forth poems. The difference in human birth is just that it is a physical exchange. A father's love can be just as intense as a mother's.

Birth and death deal with specific incidents confined by time. It seems to me that the more diffuse nature of love must make it a more demanding theme. Birth and death were dominant themes in your first three books. Do you think the fact that the new volume is called Love Poems *indicates a progression?*

I hadn't thought of it quite like that, but I suppose you are right. I do think it is harder to write well about love. In some ways the love poems are all a celebration of touch—that's the name of the first poem—but physical and emotional touch. It is a very physical book.

Why do you say in your poem "The Black Art," "when we marry, the children leave in disgust," referring to women writers?

Actually, I was referring to two writers who marry, and then divorce. I don't think that two writers often make satisfactory parents. Children need one parent who is normal. What I mean by that is that one of the characteristics of a writer is his childlike quality. Perhaps that's what my children mean when they say they'd like a "regular mommy." They are reacting to the childlike side of me. They probably also mean someone who spends more time than I do baking chocolate chip cookies.

How old are your daughters?

Twelve and fourteen.

Do they read your poetry?

Sometimes—they read the poems about themselves.

How do they react?

I think they take it for granted. They've grown up with it. Just lately they have started to dislike it. They want to be themselves and don't like to be interviewed and photographed. It's understandable.

Are people in general influenced in their attitude to you by the way you write?

Yes. People are always afraid of writers. They always expect to be written about. It's like talking to a psychoanalyst at a cocktail party. You always imagine he's analyzing you, and of course he's not. It is different with writers though, for in a sense they never take time off. They are always listening to words. I often say to my friends: "Can I have that?" I find people are often nervous with me. They think I'm some kind of weird asylum drop-out, but then they find I'm quite ordinary and they are surprised.

With Lois Ames

Anne Sexton of Weston, who won the Pulitzer Prize for Poetry in 1967, has begun a new career—as a playwright. Her play, "Mercy Street," opened last night at St. Clement's Church, 423 West 46th Street, New York City, which houses the American Place Theater.

During a break in rehearsals, Anne talked about the play, its origins, and her reactions to her new role with Lois Ames. Here are excerpts from their tape-recorded conversation.

Why don't we start by talking about Mercy Street. *What I have told people is that it really encompasses the great themes of the twentieth-century American in the third part of the century: sex . . .*

There's sex in it, of course.

And psychiatry, and religion, and money . . .

Once the director said, "It's a play about money."

And the evolution of American women . . .

I'm not sure about Daisy, the heroine, but she has a great-aunt, a Victorian woman who had a career, who worked on a newspaper. A very dominant female.

Boston Sunday Herald Traveler Book Guide, October 12, 1969. Reprinted with permission of the *Boston Herald*.

Really a "bluestocking" of her era.

Yes, but the heroine in the play looks for Christ and goes back through her life.

Don't you think Daisy is a freer, more open human being than the great-aunt?

Oh, yes, she's a woman of our generation. The play is staged in 1969 during a Mass and a psychiatrist-priest is the girl's central support.

How did the play evolve?

Four or five years ago I received a Ford Foundation grant to write for the theater. I was in residence with the Charles Playhouse in Boston, and I wrote a play which was then titled *Tell Me Your Answer True,* and the Charles Playhouse gave it a little bit of work, not very much. And then I put it away, thanked my agent, and nothing ever came of it. Later, in a *Paris Review* interview, I said that I hated the theater, and that I was very sour. Sour because I had never been produced. Then this spring the American Place Theater in New York got interested in the play, and they agreed to give a "staged reading." They worked on it for two weeks. I did a lot of rewriting then, and changed the title to *Mercy Street.* When they decided to make the play their first production this fall, I worked all summer on it. Now we're in New York at rehearsals, rewriting and working it out.

But actually, the genesis of Mercy Street *was not when you received the Ford Grant. The germ of the play had been with you years earlier.*

Well, before that the Charles Playhouse had a writers' workshop kind of thing and different writers and actors would go in, oh, maybe fifteen people, to a loft on Berkeley Street over the Hotel Diplomat. It was once a church. They gave readings of people's scripts. At the end of the evening, they would pass the hat around and everyone would put some money in it. I went with a friend of mine who was writing a play.

Who was the friend?

Eleanor Boylan, who is director of the Young Newton Players and a puppeteer. I went with her, and was quite interested in what they were doing. And then I thought, "Gee, maybe I could write a play," so I started a few scenes, and I brought them in and they read them, and I put my money in the hat.

Was this after you published To Bedlam and Part Way Back *and* All My Pretty Ones?

Yes, I was in the middle of *Live or Die.*

For which you got the Pulitzer Prize in 1967. Tell me, what was the central theme of that first play?

Christ and madness. A girl who has committed suicide finds herself in death as a character in a circus sideshow looking for Christ. She is hounded by morality figures with names like Backbiter, Barker, Flesh, and Charity and when she turns from religion to psychiatry, she finds no Christ in that realm either.

The American Place Theater gave you a staged reading this spring. When you were on the Ford grant at the Charles Playhouse, did you ever have any kind of staging of this play, or any of its scenes?

About two scenes, but they were never staged. I learned a lot from it. I was working with the director, Ben Shaktman, and he was a great help to me, helped me rewrite one certain scene, going over it and over it, and helping me with it a lot.

Oh, you never actually saw your characters?

I only saw five minutes of the morality figures.

I see. And these are the people you have so transmuted at this point that they really are not recognizable from the original script?

No, none of what was at the Charles remains. What I worked on with Ben just by letter does remain, just one little scene.

I see. How long did you work on it before that—in the loft?

Oh, that was about two weeks.

I see; and then how long was it worked on at the Charles Playhouse?

I can't remember. I think that same year of the loft I was nominated for the Ford grant, and then you have to wait, you know, to see if you're going to get it. And I said, "One thing I'll do if you give me this grant is write a play," and actually, before I got the grant—I think I got it in September—I had written a version of the play. During July—June and July—I worked oh, constantly, I didn't sleep at all. And I didn't take care of my family or anything. I just worked on the play.

And then after you got the Ford grant did you work on it . . .

I was still by myself. I was just going to the Charles Playhouse, and they were rehearsing things, other things . . .

For consultation . . .

No, I was just going to watch how it took place.

I see. You were really being exposed to the theater, learning its tricks . . .

I find now, in the theater, that I didn't learn enough.

And that went on for how many months?

During the whole season.

Then at the end of the season you hoped that the play might be produced somewhere, and it wasn't.

I sent it to my agent and nothing happened.

Now, this must have been about 1964, I would suspect?

I would say that's a pretty good guess.

By the time I met you, you had completely given up the idea of ever writing a play, and as late as last February you handed me a light blue folder, saying to me, "You've read my successes. Since you're my biographer,* you'd better take a look at this, because this is one of my failures—I have failures, too." And I took it home and read it and remember being so excited and calling you the next morning and telling you it wasn't a failure, it just needed a lot of cutting and rewriting. It's such a different play now, in September, from what it was in February.

Yes, it certainly is.

And so many people have contributed to it, to the work on it, and yet all of it has come out of you.

First I have my ideas. Then the producer has ideas, then the director has ideas . . .

But it's all going through you, the poet-playwright, it's all shunted through you and you act almost as a vessel. I think you do this with poetry, but it's more immediate now, watching you write a play. Do you remember the day we went to the Church of the Advent in Boston?

It was suggested by the producer, Wynn Handman (who is the director of The American Place), that we set *Mercy Street* in an Episcopal church while Daisy is taking communion. And that was very much to my mind because the play has a great deal to

---

*This is no longer the case.—ED.

do with Christ and yet it isn't essentially Roman Catholic. And you and I decided to go to church. You found the Church of the Advent on Brimmer Street for us, and Father Collingwood, who said, "You'll see the greatest show ever . . ." We loved it. The music, the incense and all of it. It was very dramatic. [. . .]

I think it's fair to say that you have disemboweled the Mass and siphoned it into your play chunk by chunk. Of course, theater began in the church. And the first version of your play used morality figures. Now Mercy Street *is opening on October 11 at St. Clement's Church here in New York. Why don't we talk for a moment about your reaction the first time you saw your play on the stage? I saw your excitement at seeing your words become three-dimensional, become people.*

Oh, it was wonderful! I mean it was a thrill to hear other people read it, instead of me alone in my study, reading aloud.

And you kept pushing everyone toward production . . .

Well, I wasn't sure, I was hopeful. You know, one thing, I loathe the thought of audiences coming in. I think I want them just to do it for me.

Why?

I don't have any idea—you see, it'll be such an exposure of me. Though I'm known for that in my poetry, for some reason I feel more vulnerable in the play. Of course, I've read to audiences many times, but that's something I never enjoyed anyway, giving readings. But somehow the idea of an audience there—I don't know, maybe when they come in I'll love it. If they like it I'll be happy. I just have this horror that maybe they'll avert their eyes and say, "Oh, no."

Do you find it a cathartic experience?

I keep thinking it ought to make some great psychic change in me to watch these actors relive part of my life.

Do you think it has made any kind of psychic change?

I think it has. I think I'm stronger.

I think so, too.

But I'm not sure that's due to the play; maybe it's that I am finding I can handle myself in New York and I'm a little less of a country girl. I like to tell people I'm a country girl. But now I'm a little surer of myself. And there's a thrill working with those people, instead of the isolation of the poet. They're warm. They're intuitive. They're not boxed in.

You have so much talent and intelligence at your disposal. And there is a camaraderie in the group working on the production. Significant changes have been made in the play, even since the staged reading.

We keep making changes, and I come back to the hotel room and rewrite, and I am sure we'll continue to make changes.

What happens to you when you are writing a play that is different from writing a poem?

Depends on the poem. A lot of my poems are monologues, or even dialogues. Often, I become someone else in a poem. It's very much like writing a play, because I become that person. I wrote a poem once about Christ waking up in the tomb after he had been crucified.

"In the Deep Museum."

Yes. And I spent about two months thinking about Christ, and how he would speak, and I got to the point where I even believed I was Christ, in order to write that—not with my rational mind, but with my emotional sensibility, I became

Christ. Then I wrote a monologue. Well, with the play, I became each person—I love doing this. I think it's something I can do, too. I do it pretty well. I become someone else. I tell their story. I love to write in the first person, even when it isn't about me, and it's quite confusing to my readers, because they think everything I write—sometimes I am talking about myself and sometimes not.

In what way is writing a play different from writing poetry?

It's so much larger. There's a lot of Scotch tape and scissors. A play takes every minute of your time, every ounce of your energy. It's like balancing . . . or juggling ten balls and keeping them up. You have to be aware of every person you're writing about, every character, all at once.

What do you mean, aware of them?

Well, you *are* them.

You know, you're so happy these days. I've never seen you so happy.

I've got a cast. Once you stop writing the play and start getting the actors, that's the satisfying part, because it's collaboration. I like the interaction, the excitement of it, the bouncing of ideas, the mounting of emotion that goes on. Writing poetry is a solitary act. Writing a play is a community program. Not in the initial writing, but the subsequent writing.

What are your plans for the future? How do you feel about the theater now?

I love it. I think when I am here that I could write another play.

Of course, you will.

And I don't think I'll make as many mistakes the second time. But maybe I will. I understand the theater a bit better now.

What do you understand about the theater now?

Well, you can write a play like you're writing a movie. You don't have to worry about how people move around or how they get in and out or how it will work, because that's the director's problem. My problem is only in writing it, making speech. I think I'll be freer, maybe a little wilder, as I became with this play finally.

Have you ever considered doing a movie?

I don't know how, but probably it's the same thing.

One of the things that struck me this summer and fall is that you have become very tough. You've given up parts, some of the characters, some of the passages, some of the events in this play that you clung to for four years. It's been like watching some creature shed skin after skin.

Like a surgeon, right down to the bone. That's why I liked it. My method in writing a poem is to expand, expand, expand, and then slice, and then expand, then slice, then expand, then slice, cut. And that's the way it always works. So playwriting is just done on a larger scale. I expand, then I cut. I don't mind cutting things. People have said about my poetry, "How could you cut those lines? They're good." But they're never really lost, they're on a worksheet. I might use them in another poem. And there are millions more. I mean the well never goes dry. I mean, you bubble up with ideas. And if you cut them off it's shaping, it's kind of like carving on a statue, trying to get down to the bone. You just leave the bare essentials.

Anne, you've had many grants. What was your first grant?

I got a grant from the Radcliffe Institute for Independent Study, and it was the most exciting grant I ever got, because I had never gotten anything and I wasn't very respected by my friends, or my acquaintances, or even my family, and most importantly my cleaning woman. They all thought that I was doing nothing but conning away at the typewriter and being very silly. When I got that recognition and that money, they started to give me a little privacy and respect for what I was trying to do.

You're staying in New York while this is being worked on and produced. You have a Guggenheim grant.

Yes, I'm on a Guggenheim, which has helped me afford to be able to be here, because life in New York, even my simple living, is quite expensive.

Tell me what your New York working day is like.

Well, you wake up about eight o'clock and you have breakfast, and then you go to the theater at ten. You break at one until two o'clock for lunch, then you work until six-thirty. Some days we work until ten at night. It's very grueling for me. I lead a very quiet life in Weston and a lot more energy is required of me here in New York.

Yet you recognize that it is essential to be here.

Yes, because I might be needed. You never know which second they are going to turn to you and say, "Now Anne, what do you mean by that?" Sometimes I read the cast poems to show them what something means, or I give them more background on a section of the play or tell them what a character of seventy felt as a child. And I've been rewriting whole scenes when they didn't go right. I've been doing an awful lot of cutting, changing.

There are times in life when one stands aside and watches oneself. It was fun listening to you as you sat at your desk in your yellow wrapper, beating your typewriter and saying, "Look at me, Lois, it's too funny, just like the movies—steaming hot outside, we've just limped across Times Square, the air conditioner's set on high, and here I am, the playwright, back at the Algonquin, rewriting the play. It's just like the movies!"

It's fun. I love it.

Most of the actors knew your work well before they came into this play; some of them came to Mercy Street simply because they knew that you were the writer. They had never read the play. They took it on faith, because it was Anne Sexton's play.

It's unbelievable to me that I am that well-known. I couldn't believe it. It always amazes me when strangers have read my poetry.

At one point Wynn Handman said to you, "The words will go beyond you, the play will become the actors' and director's, eventually the audience's play . . . the words will become the world's." How do you feel about that?

I don't know. It scares me. At the rehearsals, I'm just the writer, I don't know everything. I feel like a carpenter who maybe was building a cathedral and had little to do with it. I don't even feel like the architect, just the carpenter. What it will do after it goes beyond me has nothing to do with me.

With William Heyen and Al Poulin

One day during the summer of 1962 or 1963 I was browsing through magazines in the Ohio University library—I was in graduate school and had begun to write a little, very little and very badly, and I used to walk through the stacks of periodicals hoping that one day I would have a poem in one of those magazines—when I happened to read a review in, I believe, the Kenyon Review, *of Anne Sexton's* To Bedlam and Part Way Back. *I didn't pay much attention to what was being said about her, but I remember that I was amazed by the lines the critic quoted. There were sharp, brilliant images like no others I'd ever seen. I'd not at this point read or even heard of* Heart's Needle *or* Life Studies, *and this woman, Sexton, was making poems out of personal materials in a way that astounded me. As I write this, I still have an impression of the vivid color and precision I felt as I read her lines; I still recall being stunned by the truth-telling power of those early cries of hers.*

I never followed through, I guess, never had time to give myself to her. The following several years blurred into study and teaching. Graduate school involved immersing myself in sometimes three or four different centuries during the same semester; teaching was often a battle to get something read a week ahead of my students. In about 1970 I began using some of Sexton's poems from anthologies in classes, and during the dreary winter of 1971–72, in Germany with

---

American Poets in 1976, edited by William Heyen (Indianapolis: Bobbs-Merrill, 1976). Reprinted with permission.

130

my family, at the same time that I was reading stories from the Penguin edition of Grimm's Fairy Tales *to our children, I ordered the limited edition of her* Transformations. *I was happy to get Anne's book, which came boxed in mauve and with gilt edges, proper and gaudy apparel for a* tour-de-force *of a book by a remarkable woman.*

She came to Brockport for a reading on September 10, 1973. I'd written her about writing something for this book, and the first thing she said to me was something like "You're the one who wrote me about doing an essay, but no, no, I can't, I just can't write essays." But I liked her immediately. She was warm and friendly. She had a beautiful voice, I thought, and a laugh that made me feel at ease. I nagged her into signing some books for me, and began to feel relieved about the television tape Al Poulin and I were to make with her. I knew she would be easy to talk to. I enjoyed her company. The three of us spent almost the whole next day, the day of the reading, sipping drinks in the dark of a Brockport bar. After her fine reading that evening, I heard from students for weeks about how bowled over they had been by her poems and by her honesty and just by her presence.

What follows is a transcription of the hour-long videotaped interview that took place the following morning. I have not tried to make this transcription any more elegant than was our conversation. It is filled with hesitancies, and in the case of Anne Sexton, particularly, her voice makes transitions in subtle ways not readily apparent in the printed words. I've used dots to indicate pauses, passing time, not ellipsis. Nothing is left out. I've tried, with commas and dashes, to catch the intention behind the staccato of her speech.

With Anne's permission and blessing, I was transcribing this interview for the beautiful little magazine Strivers' Row. *I hovered about half finished—the fate of that magazine, which has since folded, was in doubt—when news of her death reached Brockport. At her reading, talking about her abandoned idea of saving her "Furies" poems for a posthumous book, she had said: "It suddenly occurred to me, 'Well, Sexton, someday you're gonna die, and there'll be nothing, I mean, and wouldn't it be nice if there'd be a book that would come out?'" Well, there will be books, including books of her own, but she would have been happy, I know, to be here in this volume among so many of her friends.*

Well, then, here we were, Al and I, with Anne in the studio, very nervous, on September 11, 1973. Cued, she begins by speaking into a camera directly in front of her. [W. H.]

Sexton: I'd like to read a poem from my second book, *All My Pretty Ones*. It was in response to a letter from a friend in Japan, who is since deceased. I introduce it by saying "For my friend, Ruth, who urges me to make an appointment for the Sacrament of Confession." The title is

With Mercy for the Greedy

Concerning your letter in which you ask
me to call a priest and in which you ask
me to wear The Cross that you enclose;
your own cross,
your dog-bitten cross,
no larger than a thumb,
small and wooden, no thorns, this rose—

I pray to its shadow,
that gray place
where it lies on your letter . . . deep, deep.
I detest my sins and I try to believe
in The Cross. I touch its tender hips, its dark jawed face,
its solid neck, its brown sleep.

True. There is
a beautiful Jesus.
He is frozen to his bones like a chunk of beef.
How desperately he wanted to pull his arms in!
How desperately I touch his vertical and horizontal axes!
But I can't. Need is not quite belief.

All morning long
I have worn
your cross, hung with package string around my throat.
It tapped me lightly as a child's heart might,
tapping secondhand, softly waiting to be born.
Ruth, I cherish the letter you wrote.

My friend, my friend, I was born
doing reference work in sin, and born
confessing it. This is what poems are:
with mercy
for the greedy,
they are the tongue's wrangle,
the world's pottage, the rat's star.

*When Anne finishes reading the poem, there is music—our videotape
theme has been Joanquin Rodrigo's stately and beautiful* Concierto
de Aranjuez *by Laurindo Almeida and the Modern Jazz Quartet—
and the credits and taped introductions roll. The three of us sit
quietly. Then the mikes open again and the camera swings to Al.*

[. . .]

Poulin: Anne, the poem you just read always moves me a
great deal—especially the lines "I was born / doing reference
work in sin, and born / confessing it." Do you still feel that
poetry is confession?

Sexton: Well, for a while, oh for a long while, perhaps even
now, I was called a "confessional poet." And for quite a while
I resented it. You know, I thought "Why am I in this bag?"
And then I kind of looked around and I thought "Look,
Anne, you're the *only* confessional poet around." I mean I
don't see anyone else quite doing this sort of thing. And then
as years go by I get into new themes, etcetera, etcetera, and
really don't think about what I am. You know, it shifts,
anyway.

Poulin: If it is confession, what are you confessing?

Sexton: Well, I've got to say it's not exactly, I mean it's a diffi-
cult label, "confessional," because I'll often confess to things

that never happened. As I once said to someone, if I did all the things I confess to, there would be no time to write a poem. So, you know, I mean I'll often assume the first person and it's someone else's story. It's just very amenable to me to kind of climb into that persona and tell their story.

Poulin: Were the early poems in *All My Pretty Ones* and *To Bedlam*—the poems about madness—were they real poems about madness? Or were they poems about real madness?

Sexton: I don't think I was ever really mad. I mean . . . but then again, of course, perhaps I was, but it depends on the clinical evaluation, really. "Mad" is an open term. But they were about my . . . they were confession, let us put it that way. I mean they were my experiences, some of my experiences, about feelings, disorientation, mental hospitals, whatever, and I got that label very early, the "mad poet" and all that. And at one point just a short while ago I said "I shall never again write about a psychiatrist, a madhouse, or anything to do with those themes." But, you know, of course you can't really predict, you just make these little predictions.

Heyen: Someone said that *no one,* in the history of our poetry, has ever "reported" (I think that was the word) as much of the self as has Anne Sexton. And I think, when we look back, that it really is true, that there's so much of yourself coming out in *To Bedlam* and in the later books that we never did have anything quite like this in English poetry before. How did this come about? James Wright said about *To Bedlam and Part Way Back,* Al, "The book is a work of genius. It signifies a moment of major importance to American literature." And I think it does! We've really not had that kind of poetry ever before. Where did this, how did this breakthrough come about, that you could sit down and write these sorts of poems?

Sexton: I will tell you as exactly as I can. The fact is I couldn't help it. It's just natural to me. I was told over and over: "You can't write personal poems; you can't write about madness; you can't do this." Everybody I consulted said "Nix. You don't write about that, that's not a theme." Which I never understood. And I remember something I never understood, one of my first teachers, John Holmes, saying (and I'll probably get this wrong so forgive the misquote) that Richard Wilbur said poetry is a window, not a door. And apparently, I guess, I was the door, or something. . . .

Heyen: Yes.

Sexton: But I thought, well, I'm sorry, I can only do what I can do, and it was, you know, just natural. It was not a planned thing to come into English poetry, which I didn't even know—I was just writing, and what I was writing was what I was feeling, and that's what I needed to write.

I want to go on a little bit to say I have a new little theory. Now, it may change in a month or something, but this theory is that if you could document—I don't mean "document" because it's not altogether documentary, of course—but if you could document the imagination, experiences, everything, even some wit, whatever, of one life, one life, however long it may last, it might be of some value to someone someday just to say, well, this human being lived from 1928 to whenever, and this is what she had to say about her life. And that's really all I know. I don't know anything more cosmic, anyway, so I might as well stick with what I . . .

Heyen: Would you take that a step further and not only say that maybe people will look back and say here is one life and what we can learn from it, but that here is one life that also speaks about our own lives? You see, that would be in the Whitmanian . . .

Sexton: Well, that's the idea, the attempt, but it's not a very conscious attempt—rather, it's a conscious attempt, conscious thought, or rationale for what is only natural and I can't help doing anyway, so what the hell. I mean, one formulates something that has nothing really to do with the fact that one *has* to write that way.

Heyen: To follow up one of Al's questions, and this is a much-asked question, too, but to what extent are you fictionalizing Anne Sexton as you write some of these poems? Can you say anything about that shaky ground?

Sexton: Well, there's enough fiction so that it's total confusion if one were to. . . . I remember Ralph Mills talking about my dead brother whom I've written about. And I met Ralph and I said, "Ralph,"—this was a critical essay he'd written—"Ralph, I had no brother, but then didn't we all have brothers who died in that war?" Which was the Second World War, which is a long, a few wars ago. But didn't we all, somehow, have brothers? But I write *my* brother, and of course he believes it. I mean, why not? Why shouldn't he? But I was just telling him, incidentally, there was no brother. So, that kind of . . . I should say "Excuse me, folks, but no brother," but that would kind of ruin the poem, so . . .

Poulin: This is part of that fine line between life, or reality, and art, anyway, isn't it, all the time? The discussion about writing about your own experiences always reminds me of Stevens in "The Comedian as the Letter C" where he speaks of making "his own fate an instance of all fate," which is what you were saying.

Sexton: Only he was saying it better.

Heyen: The trouble sometimes is that the so-called confessional poet *seems* to want to draw us in and say "Here I am, and I'm baring myself and I want to tell you about myself." And then on the other hand Anne Sexton writes a poem about her brother and then we feel sort of foolish when we find out, well, this is *that* kind of brother, the archetypal brother, everyone's brother rather than the real brother. It sort of makes us nervous because we like to have our feet on the ground at the same time.

Sexton: Yes, I understand, reality is always important. I think it rather pleases me in a quizzical fashion to do this because then I don't have to really admit to anything. You know, it leaves me room to say any damned thing and say, well—not actually to lie about it, for instance, to someone, but—

Heyen: It leaves the reader with the poem, too, which is probably where he should be, and not with some biographical account.

Poulin: I'd like to go back a couple of steps. When you first started writing and when people were telling you that you couldn't write like that, who *did* tell you you *could* write that way?

Sexton: All right, I can tell you exactly. First I read it—well, I'll try to explain it more clearly. I'm writing away and I'm getting acceptances and I'm getting a book oh about three-quarters finished, and, you know, the general magazines have accepted things despite all this adverse criticism, and I read in an anthology, W. D. Snodgrass's "Heart's Needle," and I think, "That's it!" And at that moment my daughter was not living at home—she was living with my mother-in-law because it was felt I was not well enough to take care of her—it was kind of a power struggle I won't go into—but I ran up and got my daughter. I said, "I must have my daughter, I've just read this poem about the loss of a daughter, etcetera." And I wrote at that time "Unknown Girl in the Maternity Ward," which is a mask—in other words, I think that's the title of it, is about having an illegitimate child and giving it away, in other words about the loss of a daughter. And as a matter of fact I had met a girl in a mental hospital who had done just this and I was projecting, I was fictionalizing, but of course, I mean, so-called confessing. At any rate, I wrote that poem, got my daughter, and what could be more beautiful than a poem to move you to action of such a type? And I thought, *this* is the thing, I like this, this is for me, boy, etcetera, and so I kind of nosed around and found out that Snodgrass would be at a writer's conference—it was a five-day one or something at Antioch—and I did go out there, and he *definitely* encouraged me, and read that poem about the loss of a daughter, that kind of fictionalized poem, and he said, "Why don't you tell the real story?" You know, he drew me out about my life. And so I spent the next seven months writing "The Double Image," which is all about many varied themes—about madness, the loss of a daughter, mother's cancer, loss of mother, regaining of daughter, and it's a long narrative piece written in very tight form.

Heyen: A lot of poets point to Snodgrass as someone who showed the way to a large extent. His poem, too, is written in very tight metrics.

Sexton: Yes, I don't think mine is quite that tight.

Heyen: You know, later on in his next book he would write poems about his daughter and he would say something like "We go about our business; /I have turned my back." So I'm a little nervous when you say it's wonderful to have a poem move us to that sort of action. Because then, speaking logically, you'd have to read his next book and then like turn your back on your daughter.

Sexton: I see. But it would only be action that is ready to be born within you, that is right there, and yet the poem lets it rise and brings you forth and out you go. I mean . . .

Heyen: Yes, I see, I see.

Poulin: Would you mind reading the unknown girl poem?

Sexton: I suppose I could read it, yeah. I don't feel it's—I'm worried that it's not too well written. It's an early, early poem, but we'll skip that and read it.

Unknown Girl in the Maternity Ward

Child, the current of your breath is six days long.
You lie, a small knuckle on my white bed;
lie, fisted like a snail, so small and strong
at my breast. Your lips are animals; you are fed
with love. At first hunger is not wrong.
The nurses nod their caps; you are shepherded
down starch halls with the other unnested throng
in wheeling baskets. You tip like a cup; your head
moving to my touch. You sense the way we belong.
But this is an institution bed.
You will not know me very long.

The doctors are enamel. They want to know
the facts. They guess about the man who left me,
some pendulum soul, going the way men go
and leave you full of child. But our case history
stays blank. All I did was let you grow.
Now we are here for all the ward to see.
They thought I was strange, although
I never spoke a word. I burst empty
of you, letting you learn how the air is so.
The doctors chart the riddle they ask of me
and I turn my head away. I do not know.

Yours is the only face I recognize.
Bone at my bone, you drink my answers in.
Six times a day I prize
your need, the animals of your lips, your skin
growing warm and plump. I see your eyes
lifting their tents. They are blue stones, they begin
to outgrow their moss. You blink in surprise
and I wonder what you can see, my funny kin,
as you trouble my silence. I am a shelter of lies.

Should I learn to speak again, or hopeless in
such sanity will I touch some face I recognize?

Down the hall the baskets start back. My arms
fit you like a sleeve, they hold
catkins of your willows, the wild bee farms
of your nerves, each muscle and fold
of your first days. Your old man's face disarms
the nurses. But the doctors return to scold
me. I speak. It is you my silence harms.
I should have known; I should have told
them something to write down. My voice alarms
my throat. "Name of father—none." I hold
you and name you bastard in my arms.

And now that's that. There is nothing more
that I can say or lose.
Others have traded life before
and could not speak. I tighten to refuse
your owling eyes, my fragile visitor.
I touch your cheeks, like flowers. You bruise
against me. We unlearn. I am a shore
rocking you off. You break from me. I choose
your only way, my small inheritor
and hand you off, trembling the selves we lose.
Go child, who is my sin and nothing more.

Poulin: That's a very moving poem. Hearing you read it,
threw me. . . . One of the things that strikes me is that the
poem is very tightly structured and many of your early poems
are in rather traditional form.

Sexton: Well, I wouldn't put it that way. Form, but usually not
traditional. If I could explain: I think, or at least thought
when I was writing these poems in form that it was *my* form,
you know? Not that I made it up, of course—that would be
impossible. [. . .] I found that the more difficult the subject,
then the easier it was to do in some difficult form. [. . .] I'd
begin, say, with rhyme, and then I'd count it out syllabically,

maybe, and then I was stuck with it, and then I often broke it and cheated, [. . .] because what I was trying to get out was the honest, the truth. [. . .] It took over the superego function. In other words, there's something saying "You can't do this, so don't worry about it, it's impossible." So, that took over that problem, and so it could come forth.

Heyen: Now the superego took over what problem?

Sexton: That I can't say this, I can't find the truth, I don't know what I'm about to reveal or say or do. [. . .]

Heyen: You probably feel that a poem takes you where it sort of has to go, and you don't feel critically conscious, one step ahead of . . .

Sexton: Well, I never do, anyway . . .

Heyen: You once said that you considered your poems primitive, rather than intellectual.

Sexton: That's because people have told me that and I thought it sounded so nice that I'd go along with it. First of all, I'm not an intellectual of any sort that I know of. I have many friends who are intellectuals, whatever that word means exactly, but primitive, yes, because I didn't know a damn thing about poetry! Nothing! I had never gone to college, I absolutely was a flunk-out in any schooling I had, I laughed my way through exams. You know. They just kind of passed me on, but, you know, nothing came through. I don't know the multiplication table, can't spell, can't punctuate. And until I started at twenty-seven, hadn't done much reading. Oh, yes, well, of course, some, but not much, and certainly not in poetry. So I was just what one would call a primitive. . . . And, unfortunately, bad for me, I wasn't reading enough, I was writing too much. You know, I mean if I'd just told myself to put the typewriter away for a while and read up and see what's going on. . . .

Poulin: Do you struggle over poems?

Sexton: Some.

Poulin: It depends on what the poem is?

Sexton: Yes. I mean we all have, you know the term, the "given" poem. I mean that happens once in a great while and one says "Thank you, thank you, how nice of you." But, I'm afraid I'm getting, I don't know, lazy or, I don't know what it is.

Heyen: Do you mean poems seem to be fewer and further between?

Sexton: No, no, increasing at a great rate.

Heyen: Oh, I see. Yes, well someone said about Wallace Stevens that at the end of his life he found out what a Wallace Stevens poem was supposed to sound like and he sort of went ahead and wrote them out, so maybe . . .

Sexton: Well, I don't know, I don't have any feeling like that. As a matter of fact, I'm always trying to write something that doesn't, you know, that isn't, or—I don't even know what an Anne Sexton poem sounds like, unless I should read some sort of imitation I might kind of catch on—but I don't know really what I'm doing or what I sound like. I guess the only thing I really do know is that I have a great feeling for imagery. I mean it to me is the heart of the poem, and without it . . .

Heyen: These questions about—when do you write and how much do you write and how much work is it—they all sound trite but they're all very interesting to me because it seems to me that one can be very happy when he or she *manages* to write. [. . .] I'd like to find some way to be able to write a great deal, but I'm very crotchety myself, and Al, you go through long dry periods.

Sexton: But everyone does!

Heyen: If we could just find some way to write a lot.

Sexton: I went through a *long* dry period and since then it's just been *brmmmmmm* [. . .] I did do one strange thing, but it's—for a future—two books from now—but for a book which I think will be called *The Awful Rowing Toward God*. And I wrote it in two and a half weeks. . . .

Poulin: The whole book?

Sexton: Yes, but I didn't know really—this was a strange experience because [. . .] there was no time, at this just strange moment of my life, which was of great pressure emotionally— here were these poems coming, five, six, seven or whatever they were a day, and I happened to talk to John Brinnin, who is on the faculty at B.U. with me, and he said "Oh let them come, you can always fix them up later." Well I'm in a hell of a lot of trouble now because I've never operated that way. I don't quite know, well, what to do with these things. You know, it's like rewriting someone else's work, or something. But I haven't faced it yet. I mean this was just a rare occasion. I've *never* done anything like that before, and it's ridiculous to say you can write a book in two and a half weeks! That's a big laugh. So, the rewrite, who knows how long that will take?

Poulin: Were those poems some of them that appeared in *Salmagundi*?

Sexton: They've appeared nowhere.

Poulin: Oh, they haven't appeared.

Sexton: No, no, they are *unfinished*, I mean, [. . .] a few people have seen them but they're not ready for any publication because, you know, [. . .] there are flaws all over the place. I've done a little work on them but, preliminary work.

Poulin: What got you interested in doing the *Transformations?*

Sexton: Well, I just had a play off-Broadway, which I wasted about one year writing, and another year going through re-writes and hanging around New York, and going through that, and I don't quite remember the reviews, but they were kind. [. . .] Then there was this huge blank period, you know, dead, [. . .] and a friend of mine, Maxine Kumin is writing a poem about her daughter, and we talk over our poems all the time, workshop them, you know, on the phone or—she lives close to me—and I don't really remember if I led her to the theme of Snow White or she did—I don't really recall, but she said "I've forgotten," and so I call my daughter Linda to the phone and I said "Honey, will you read *Snow White* to Maxine?" [. . .] So I hear this and little sparks go and I think, "I wonder if this is something I might. . . ." I was very vague, and I'd try a little introductory poem, and then I'd [try] another, and I still don't know what I'm doing, but. . . . Then I think—I've written about three, say—and I say "Well I don't know what I'm doing, but—if you could do *Snow White*, Anne, after Disney and all that, and make it something that's yours, and Snow White's, and the Queen's and the cast, then you've got it licked." [. . .] My daughter would—I've forgotten her age at the time, she may have been seventeen, I don't really remember, I mean I could count back, but, I think about seventeen or sixteen—at any rate, she'd say "Why don't you try"—because she also obsessionally read these tales—not as long, but—it was her book I worked from, Modern Library edition, you know, I don't know what edition I had as a child, but. . . .

Heyen: I like those poems very much, especially the *Rumpelstiltskin* poem. . . .

Sexton: Yes.

Heyen: They're a lot of fun, and they're also scary at the same time, "The Frog Prince," and . . .

Sexton: Well, what my real joy was was to read—sometimes my daughter would suggest "read this or that, try this one" or something, you know, or—and if I got, as I was reading it, some unconscious message that I had something to say, what I had fun with were the prefatory things, I mean that's where I got my great kicks, where I expressed whatever it evoked in me—and it had to evoke something in me or I couldn't do it. Now they all came rather quickly except for "Sleeping Beauty," which took me three months. [. . .]

Poulin: Yes, and you went out beyond the fairy tales, also, didn't you? Because "The Little Peasant," for example is . . .

Sexton: "The Little Peasant" is right in there. That's a Grimm's fairy tale.

Poulin: Is it? I thought it was from Chaucer.

Sexton: Well, you know, things float around. But it was in that book, if one can believe it, and of course one can't, so. . . .

Poulin: But did you embellish it? [. . .]

Sexton: Oh, yes, I embellished it, oh, indeed, it wasn't that way.

Poulin: It's no longer a child's story.

Sexton: None of them are children's stories.

Poulin: I suppose we should ask you to read that one, since we have talked about it.

Sexton: It takes a while, but if you'd like, I'd be glad to.

Poulin: Sure. That's a fun one, also.

Sexton: Yeah. . . . It's an unfamiliar one. Most people don't know it, but. . . . It's got a long kind of prefatory thing, and I'll tell you when I begin the story—the way I happen to retell it, which is with a few added features.

The Little Peasant

Oh how the women
grip and stretch
fainting on the horn.

The men and women
cry to each other.
Touch me,
my pancake,
and make me young.
And thus
like many of us,
the parson
and the miller's wife
lie down in sin.

The women cry,
Come, my fox,
heal me.
I am chalk white
with middle age
so wear me threadbare,
wear me down,
wear me out.
Lick me clean,
as clean as an almond.

The men cry,
Come, my lily,
my fringy queen,
my gaudy dear,
salt me a bird
and be its noose.
Bounce me off

like a shuttlecock.
Dance me dingo-sweet
for I am your lizard,
your sly thing.

(Now starts the story.)

Long ago
there was a peasant
who was poor but crafty.
He was not yet a voyeur.
He had yet to find
the miller's wife
at her game.
Now he had not enough
cabbage for supper
nor clover for his one cow.
So he slaughtered the cow
and took the skin
to town.
It was worth no more
than a dead fly
but he hoped for profit.

On his way
he came upon a raven
with damaged wings.
It lay as crumpled as
a wet washcloth.
He said, Come little fellow,
you're part of my booty.

On his way
there was a fierce storm.
Hail jabbed the little peasant's cheeks
like toothpicks.
So he sought shelter at the miller's house.
The miller's wife gave him only
a hunk of stale bread
and let him lie down on some straw.
The peasant wrapped himself and the raven
up in the cowhide
and pretended to fall asleep.

When he lay
as still as a sausage
the miller's wife
let in the parson, saying,
My husband is out
so we shall have a feast.
Roast meat, salad, cakes and wine.
The parson,
his eyes as black as caviar,
said, Come, my lily,
my fringy queen.
The miller's wife,
her lips as red as pimientoes,
said, Touch me, my pancake,
and wake me up.
And thus they ate.
And thus
they dingoed-sweet.

Then the miller
was heard stomping on the doorstep
and the miller's wife
hid the food about the house
and the parson in the cupboard.

The miller asked, upon entering,
What is that dead cow doing in the corner?
The peasant spoke up.
It is mine.
I sought shelter from the storm.
You are welcome, said the miller,
but my stomach is as empty as a flour sack.
His wife told him she had no food
but bread and cheese.
So be it, the miller said,
and the three of them ate.

The miller looked once more
at the cowskin
and asked its purpose.
The peasant answered,

I hide my soothsayer in it.
He knows five things about you
but the fifth he keeps to himself.
The peasant pinched the raven's head
and it croaked, Krr. Krr.
That means, translated the peasant,
there is wine under the pillow.
And there it sat
as warm as a specimen.

Krr. Krr.
They found the roast meat under the stove.
It lay there like an old dog.
Krr. Krr.
They found the salad in the bed
and the cakes under it.
Krr. Krr.

Because of all this
the miller burned to know the fifth thing.
How much? he asked,
little caring he was being milked.
They settled on a large sum
and the soothsayer said,
The devil is in the cupboard.
And the miller unlocked it.
Krr. Krr.

There stood the parson,
rigid for a moment,
as real as a soup can
and then he took off like a fire
with the wind at its back.
I have tricked the devil,
cried the miller with delight,
and I have tweaked his chin whiskers.
I will be as famous as the king.

The miller's wife
smiled to herself.
Though never again to dingo-sweet

her secret was as safe
as a fly in an outhouse.

The sly little peasant
strode home the next morning,
a soothsayer over his shoulder
and gold pieces knocking like marbles
in his deep pants pocket.
Krr. Krr.

Poulin: [. . .] It seems to me that in the progression from your
first book to your later books, including your forthcoming
Death Notebooks, that you move increasingly away from sin and
madness toward love and God. Is that a fair estimate?

Sexton: Just about, but I wouldn't leave sin alone . . . because I
would say one could have a great sense of sin and reach for
God. I mean. . . .

Heyen: This is a Pandora's box. This is on somewhat the same
subject, and I hate to ask it because you've been asked it so
often, I'm sure, and also because it's so difficult. . . . I've al-
ways felt that we can never, of course, dictate what a poet
ought to write about. I mean, that would be absolutely foolish.
At the same time—it was just a couple of weeks ago that I
read Sylvia Plath's *The Bell Jar.* And now for years I've been
reading Berryman's *Dream Songs,* that elegiac genius of his.
And I've read Anne Sexton for a long time. An awful lot of
pain and death and a preponderance of darkness in the early
books—critics have complained about it again and again.
James Wright, not talking about you but talking about the
darkness of some of his own work said he sometimes wearies
of it—"There's something also to be said for the light," he
said. How do you react when critics say something like "I wish
she'd look *out* further."? . . . You know, Richard Wilbur has a
poem on Sylvia Plath—

Sexton: I do believe I've read it . . .

Heyen: Yes, and he says that she had to sound her "brilliant negative," in poems "free, and helpless, and unjust." The last word is "unjust." And he said at a reading that, well, there's a sense in which she's being somewhat unjust to the world. And, speaking honestly, sometimes I read your early poems and it seems that *all* the women in the early poems have sagging breasts, and *all* the old men are unhappy, and I think of that word by Wilbur, "unjust," and I wondered, does poetry have to come out of that sense of pain, and the sense of darkness?

Sexton: Actually not. It comes out of wherever you are. I mean you've got to go forward and read more recent books. . . . I mean certainly that what I just read was not the pit of darkness, or despair.

Heyen: No, the *Transformations* poems are a lot of fun. And there are others in earlier books that I love—"Letter Written on a Ferry While Crossing Long Island Sound," which ends with that nice surreal image of the nuns flying away saying "Good news, good news."

Sexton: Yes, yes, and then there's a whole book of love poems, and there's a bit of joy in that, I'd say. I mean, lightness.

Heyen: Yes. This is a very difficult subject, and I never would have found myself five years ago saying what I would say now . . .

Sexton: Well maybe you only can do that because I have, you know, after all one does grow, change, evolve [. . .]

Heyen: Yes. . . . Let me on somewhat this subject read one harsh statement about *Live or Die.*

Sexton: Okay.

Heyen: This was a review by a fellow in the *Southern Review* talking about *Live or Die*. He says, he gets angry and says, "They are not poems. They are documents of modern psychiatry and their publication is a result of the confusion of critical standards in the general mind." He says that the poems finally are embarrassing and irritating. How do you react to something like that?

Sexton: I'd say please put my book down and don't bother with it! It's for someone else. [. . .] I can't do much about it, you know, so, all right, that's his critical evaluation, I respect it as such, and he's every right to think that.

Heyen: Yes, you have to go on writing what you have to write.

Sexton: Yeah.

Poulin: Another harsh statement by . . .

Sexton: Is this called harsh statement time?

Poulin: No, but it's . . .

Sexton: No, I'm kidding, come on let's get a little happy.

Poulin: Someone said, I think it was James Dickey who said that the personal poets aren't personal at all, they're very superficial, that it's only the facade of the person that's coming through. How do you respond to that?

Sexton: I think it's a goddamned lie because his poems are often personal, and I think that's one of his facades. I respect him greatly as a writer, you know, [. . .] many of his poems I admire, and if he wishes to say that about personal poems, I don't think he knows what in hell he's talking about. As a matter of fact I think he's a very confused critic. I mean, he ought just to stick with his poetry, or movies, or novels, or . . . but that's just my opinion.

Heyen: Do you pay much attention to the reviews of your books, or criticism?

Sexton: Well, I never—I think I was telling Al this last night— I've never replied to a review. I feel that somehow it's taste-less. You know, they must give their. . . . Except once. But to go on with why I don't reply, because I can remember people saying "Well I had a review of eight books in the *New York Times* and I've heard from six of them." And—this was a former teacher saying that—I thought ferchrissakes, are you supposed to run around and say "thank you?" You know, because here's someone trying to tell the truth, the way they see it, and I don't think they deserve a "thank you" or a "to hell with you." I've never written a "to hell with you." At any rate, there *was* one review in a—I don't know if it's a big or small, but an English quarterly—which was *so* loving, like "Oh Anne, Anne"—I can't remember, but it was like a love letter or something. So I did cable—I didn't know who he was, I never met or heard of him—I cabled my publisher, you know, I cabled *him* c/o my publisher, and I just said "Will you marry me?" And I got a very nice letter back, you know, I mean he was. . . . That was, that's just the only time I've ever replied, and only in that vein. But I try not to let them get me down or up! You know, depending on which way it goes. Of course the publishers care terribly, and, you know, they need good quotes, and, you know, they're running a business, and if you've got entirely—for instance *Transformations* got abso-lutely the most horrible reviews in Britain, but one, which came much later, just a little while ago. I mean things like they

153

say "like Walt" and then quote two lines "Disney, we mean, not Whitman." And then it ends, "God bless America. Ha. Ha." Etcetera. And I thought, well, I guess this didn't travel very well across the Atlantic. But it didn't get me down. It might have gotten the publishers down.

Heyen: This question fits in somewhat with what Al was asking before, and this is just a grab-bag question you might just want to throw away, because I'm sure it's too general. But it's always asked. Do you see your work as having essentially changed since you began? Is there something you can say generally about some real divisions as your books have progressed? . . . That's heavy, isn't it?

Sexton: It's heavy, but it should be able to be answered. . . . I see a progression . . . just . . . well, after *Live or Die* . . . I mean, *To Bedlam and Part Way Back:* mostly madness; *All My Pretty Ones* (*mostly,* I'm saying, because this is a great generality): death of parents, and love, and some religious poems; *Live or Die:* a mixed bag, sequentially dated as I wrote the poems, thinking, you know, live, or die; then *Love Poems:* well that's, I mean a whole book of love poems, that's certainly a step in the right direction. . . . What comes next? *Transformations.* Okay. There are two rather serious *Transformations* poems, the rest are—I didn't really mean them to be comic, I mean, I guess I did, but I mean I really didn't know what I was doing, I just did what I felt like, I was very *happy* writing those poems, I was having a good time, except for a few that gave me trouble. Then *The Book of Folly* which is really kind of a mixed bag of things. It's got a little hangover from the voice of *Transformations* with some poems called "The Jesus Papers," which are called either "blasphemous" or "devout"—it's probably blasphemous, I would say. I mean one of them my publishers forced me to take out and two friends advised me to take it out: it was "Jesus Ailing," which starts out—this is unpublished, not in the book— "There was trouble that day. / Jesus was constipated." Well they said "now look, we just can't have this," so I said "okay." But in the end of that book there's a kind of belief thing going on. One fights what one. . . . You know, it's a little war. . . .

Heyen: And now you've finished a couple of other books.

Sexton: Yes. Then comes *The Death Notebooks* which is—I'd planned, I had this crazy idea I'd publish it posthumously, you know, my friends going ha, ha, ha, as they always do— not that I was going to kill myself and bring out this book, but I thought, wouldn't it be *nice*, you know, after I was dead if there were a statement about death? [. . .] And then *The Awful Rowing Toward God,* which is about as far as I've gotten.

Heyen: We began with your poem "With Mercy for the Greedy," which talks about, I suppose it talks about your effort to come to terms with the cross, and I think it makes a statement about poetry being maybe a half-way house toward a religiousness that you can hold to. With that poem and now with—I just have the title to go by, *The Awful Rowing Toward God*—have you, have you come somewhere in regard to this religious quest, or . . . ?

Sexton: I would say I *do* in *The Awful Rowing Toward God,* and I even do to a certain degree in *The Death Notebooks.* I mean it certainly ends on, I don't know—could you say how it ends?

Poulin: Well it ends with that series of psalms, which are, praise.

Sexton: Which are praise!

Poulin: And I think even the section called "The Furies."

Sexton: Which are praise! No, well, yes, yes they are.

Poulin: And we have approximately two minutes left. I have the poem from *The Death Notebooks* that we'd like you to read as a conclusion.

Sexton: There are many fury poems. This is only one of them.

The Fury of Cocks

There they are
drooping over the breakfast plates,
angel-like,
folding in their sad wing,
animal sad,
and only the night before
there they were
playing the banjo.
Once more the day's light comes
with its immense sun,
its mother trucks,
its engines of amputation.
Whereas last night
the cock knew its way home,
as stiff as a hammer,
battering in with all
its awful power.
That theater.
Today it is tender,
a small bird,
as soft as a baby's hand.
She is the house.
He is the steeple.
When they fuck they are God.
When they break away they are God.
When they snore they are God.
In the morning they butter the toast.
They don't say much.

They are still God.
All the cocks of the world are God,
blooming, blooming, blooming
into the sweet blood of woman.

With Maxine Kumin,
Elaine Showalter, and Carol Smith

> Max and I
> two immoderate sisters,
> two immoderate writers,
> two burdeners,
> made a pact.
> To beat death down with a stick.
> To take over.
> —Anne Sexton, "The Death Baby"

This conversation [April 15, 1974] between four women is about the friendship of Maxine Kumin and Anne Sexton, a friendship which began in the late 1950s, when they studied together in a poetry workshop in Boston led by John Holmes. Because they had young children, and were often unable to get out of the house, they developed a process of "workshopping" poems on the telephone, supplying for each other both detailed criticism and warm support. Both women won Pulitzer Prizes for books of poems. Anne Sexton in 1967 for Live or Die, *and Maxine Kumin in 1973 for* Up Country: Poems of New England. *Their poetic styles are completely different; Kumin's poetry is exact, formal, intensely crafted, while Sexton wrote dramatically about breakdown and death. On October 4, 1974, Anne Sexton killed herself at her home in Weston, Massachusetts.*

We met Anne and Maxine before their poetry reading at Douglass

Women's Studies: An Interdisciplinary Journal 4 (1976). Reprinted with permission.

College, and asked to talk with them together, not in the form of a traditional interview, but more as something relaxed and spontaneous. So the reader should not expect to find any theories of art, or formal or technical problems, examined here. Instead we hear the voices of Annie and Max, taped in a motel room in New Brunswick, New Jersey, on an April afternoon, interrupting each other, joking, remembering.

Kumin: Meeting Anne was really fantastic. When I met Annie she was a little flower child, she was the ex-fashion model. She wore very spiky high heels—

Sexton: Well, that was the age.

Kumin: Yes, it was. Well, she was totally chic, and I was sort of more frumpy.

Sexton: You were the most frump of the frumps. You had your hair in a little bun.

Kumin: I was the chief frump. She was really chic and she wore flowers in her hair.

Showalter: Where did you model? I remember reading that, and then it dropped out of your blurbs.

Sexton: It's called the Hart Agency, in Boston.

Kumin: She was a Hart girl. At any rate, we met at the Boston Center for Adult Education where we had each come to study with John Holmes.

Sexton: I came trembling, thinking, oh dear god, with the most ghastly poems. Oh god, were they bad!

Kumin: Well . . . I don't know if that's true.

Sexton: Oh, oh, Maxine, horrible, horrible. Anyway, your impression of me was—?

Kumin: And my impression of Anne was—I don't know what my impression was. I was very taken with her. I think we were each very taken with each other.

Sexton: Now, wait a minute. You were scared of me.

Kumin: I was terrified of her. I had just had my closest friend commit suicide, in a postpartum depression. Gassed herself.

Sexton: I wasn't writing about that right off.

Kumin: Now, wait a minute. I'm just saying *why* I was scared.

Sexton: Why should you know I had anything to do with it?

Kumin: Well, I knew your history.

Sexton: How?

Kumin: You were very open about the fact, of why you had begun to write poetry, and how you had started to write poetry. You had just gotten out of the mental hospital. And something in me very much wanted to turn aside from this. I didn't want to let myself in for that again, for that separation. And Anne is still very much more flamboyant and open a person than I am. I'm much more closed up, restrained. I think this is certain, although much less so now than then.

Sexton: Can I say? Since your analysis—you're quite a changed person.

Kumin: Yes, since my analysis.

Sexton: I mean, she's gotten attractive and yummy. Before her hair was pulled back and in a bun—

Showalter: I wouldn't have recognized you, Maxine, from your pictures.

Sexton: No pictures are good. She was attractive then, she was attractive then; just a bad picture.

Kumin: The picture on the novel coming out next year is a really good picture of me and my dog. I recommend that picture.

Sexton: She keeps saying, look at my dog. As if the dog were more important.

Kumin: He *is* kind of spectacular. Anyway, Anne and I met, and we drove into this class together. For a long time, she used to pick me up and—

Sexton: Not at the beginning I didn't. I can remember, it was funny. I remember you going to a reading at Wellesley College and you picking me up. I had on sandals. You said, look, she has prehensile toes. I've never forgotten it. And I said, look, anytime you want me to go to a reading or anything (because I was desperate then) I'll do anything. And I started to drive Maxine to the Adult Center.

Kumin: And from that we began to go to all sorts of readings together. Actually the reading at Wellesley College was Marianne Moore.

Sexton: Remember her? Because she kept contradicting and saying, now don't handle a line this way, don't do that, that's very bad, you know, and don't end-stop here.

Kumin: She mumbled so. She read so badly. She was a character, in her tricorner hat and her great black robe.

Sexton: Do you remember going to hear Robert Graves? Dear god, he was ghastly!

Kumin: Now look, we are not here to talk about people who were ghastly readers or we'll be here all night.

Showalter: Was John Holmes in charge of that workshop?

Kumin: Yes, John Holmes was teaching a little workshop, for anybody. It was available to the world, whoever wanted to come. And we would all try our poems. And this, I think, is how Anne and I learned to work by *hearing* a poem, because we didn't bring copies. John would sit at the head of the table and shuffle through the poems.

Sexton: He didn't do anything alphabetically.

Kumin: And we would all sit there dying, hoping to be chosen.

Sexton: Oh, you'd pray to be chosen.

Showalter: Not afraid to have a poem read?

Sexton: No, not afraid, wanting to be chosen.

Kumin: And he would read your poem, and the class would then discuss it.

Sexton: And he would.

Kumin: And he would.

Sexton: Now we have to go into the fact that as it grew later— well, we used to go out afterwards. John didn't drink.

Kumin: John was a former alcoholic.

Sexton: I don't think I drank myself. I don't think I drank much *then*, really. I had a beer.

Kumin: But he was really on the wagon. He had been a severe alcoholic. And then after that we broke off from the Boston Center, and we formed our own group.

Sexton: But I didn't.

Kumin: You certainly did. When we broke off?

Sexton: I was seeing Robert Lowell.

Kumin: No, that was much later. That was after John was dead.

Sexton: No, wait a minute. I'm very sorry. I was going, to Robert Lowell's class, and still John's, without you. Begging for the approval that Daddy would never give. Why was I so masochistic?

Showalter: Was John Holmes a difficult person for a woman to work with?

Sexton: John Holmes didn't approve of a thing about me. He hated my poetry. I remember, even after Maxine had left, and I was still with Holmes, there was a new girl who came in. And he kept saying, oh, let us see *new* poems, *new* poems. We need them. And here I was giving him things that were later anthologized forever. I mean, really good poems.

Smith: Didn't Holmes write comic verse as well, himself? And think you should move in the direction of comic verse, Maxine?

Sexton: No, no, she started with comic verse.

Kumin: I had already graduated from comic verse, Carol. I had started by writing light verse; that's how I became a poet.

I started writing light verse for the slicks when I got pregnant with Danny, for a year.

Sexton: Maxine, it was two or three years, it was no one year.

Kumin: Wait a minute—he's now twenty-one. So it was twenty-one years ago. And I made a pact with myself that if I didn't sell anything by the time this child was born, I would chuck all my creative discontents. And in about my eighth month I started really landing with little four-liners, there, here and everywhere. *Saturday Evening Post* and *Cosmopolitan,* and so on. Then someone told me about John Holmes's class at the Center and in great fear and trembling I went and met Anne. We did that thing at the Center for a year and then we broke off and started a workshop of our own.

Sexton: It was at least two years.

Showalter: And who was in the second workshop?

Kumin: It consisted of Sexton, Kumin, George Starbuck, Sam Albert, and John Holmes. And for a little while, Ted Weiss.

Sexton: He was there for a while. And do you remember? the night we laughed so hard we were screaming, over women's girdles? I mean, we were hysterical. Ted Weiss was in Boston, and John wanted to bring him into the class, and he was nice. I'll never forget how we laughed. He just got us all onto women's girdles. I mean, in its own way it is a bit vulgar, and yet to me it isn't really vulgar at all. It's beauty, it's the girdle that's corrupting her. It was funny. But—I have to point this out, and you must too—John found me evil.

Kumin: But I think it should also be said, that the reason for John's reaction, we *guess,* is that his first wife had *been* mentally ill, and had killed herself.

Sexton: But I was writing about this subject. He kept saying, no no, too personal, or you musn't, or anything. Everything he said about my poems was bad, almost altogether. And yet, from the beginning, from the class, from him, I learned. And from Maxine. I must say Maxine, my best teacher—although for a while I was copying Maxine's flaws. I don't know how, I didn't know they were hers, although now I can see they were someone else's, an inversion here, or a noun. I got over that. I remember, I didn't know her very well. I wrote "Music Swims Back to Me." I was playing a record, a 45, and I was leaning over my husband who was building a hi-fi set. I was climbing over him, in the kitchen, because I wrote in the dining room—I didn't really have a place to write, I wrote on a card table—to put on the 45 again. It's necessary to hear that song, because the song was taking me back to the mental institution where it constantly played. It was a very early poem, and I had broken all my ideas of what a poem should be, and I go to Maxine—very formal—we don't know each other very well. We hadn't started writing together yet. And I said, could you—? We sat together in the living room, stiffly on the couch. Sunday. It was a Sunday. And I said, is this a poem? And she said, yes.

Kumin: Well, I get points for knowing it. I don't know how I knew it.

Sexton: She knew. She knew. She responded. I had done this crazy thing, written this poem. Always Maxine responded to my poetry. Not John, but Maxine, although in spite of herself. Because it was hard for her.

Kumin: Yes, it was hard. Here was my Christian academic daddy saying, stay away from her. She's bad for you.

Showalter: Did he actually say that?

Sexton: He would write letters saying, she's evil. He did, he said, be careful of her.

Kumin: Oh, yes, he would write me letters. He was my patron; he got me a job at Tufts.

Sexton: And for me, he was my daddy, but he was the daddy who was saying, you are no good.

Kumin: And the fantastic thing is that it did not come between us. Of course, John then died terribly, terribly. He was told that his aches and pains were mental, that he needed a psychiatrist; meanwhile he had throat cancer and it had metastasized. Had totally invaded his chest and shoulders. I remember him talking about a shawl, a cape of pain. And he started drinking again. It was awful, awful.

Sexton: It was awful. I remember calling his wife, Doris, and saying, what is it, what is it? He's not going to *die*, is he? And she said, well, it's funny, it's like psychiatry. What could she say?

Smith: Who's that?

Kumin: She was a very good foil for John, because she's very warm, very outgoing, and she supplied a lot of things that John didn't. He was really quite reserved. I thought of him as very New England.

Sexton: I remember one night Sam and me going to John's. It was sleeting out, but we make it. And he's on his way out—and he's so happy we were going out. I think maybe that moment he forgave me a little.

Kumin: I was then teaching at Tufts, but we all read at Tufts, in the David Steinman series.

Sexton: I never did. No, he wasn't going to ask *me*.

Kumin: We used to go to parties at John's after all those readings—after John Crowe Ransom, and after Robert Frost. Frost said, don't sit there mumbling in the shadows, come up here closer. By then he was very deaf. And I was so awed.

Smith: Was it out of that early relationship that you both began to work together?

Sexton: Yes, because we had to listen.

Kumin: Because we had to listen to John Holmes read the poems—copies were not provided—and then we worked together on the telephone.

Sexton: In our own workshop later we made copies. But then we worked on the phone. And sometimes my kids would be climbing all over me, and I'd say, shh! poem! Maxine! and I'd block my ear, and I could hear it. I could grasp the whole thing, and say change this, change that.

Showalter: Did you see it?

Kumin: Later. Maybe the following week, if we could get together, if one of us had a sitter.

Sexton: She means did we see it in our minds. No, no, I just knew. I could tell the poem, and I could tell what she wanted to do. We still do it.

Showalter: You don't have to anymore. This was just because you couldn't get out of the house?

Sexton: Yes, because our kids were too small.

Kumin: Yes. We did eventually do this wicked thing. We put in a second line, because our husbands complained that we were always on the phone.

Sexton: We used to talk for two hours sometimes.

Showalter: When was it that you put in the phone? Was it before or after the Radcliffe Institute?

Kumin: Probably just then, because we both probably felt flush and important.

Smith: And you would talk about each other's poems, workshop each other's poems?

Sexton: Yes, and also talk about our emotions and our feelings and what the day was like, what was going on.

Smith: When you heard each other's poems, you said before you could enter the consciousness of the other person.

Sexton: Well, you see, we never tried to make the other sound like ourselves. We always saw in the other's voice, I'm sure of it.

Kumin: We started with a recognition for and a respect for that separate identity. I would never meddle with what Anne is doing. I might be able to help her find a more effective way to do what she's doing.

Showalter: Did you ever find your own writing began to shade into the other person?

Kumin: No, no, we're different.

Sexton: You can tell we're completely different.

Showalter: Yes, but was there ever a period when there was a struggle?

Sexton: No, there was never a struggle. It was natural, it wasn't hard.

Kumin: It seems to be so normal. It wasn't ever an issue.

Sexton: There was never any struggle. Don't you see—you enter into the voice of the poet, and you think, how to shape, how to make better, but not, how to make like me.

Kumin: I think there is one conviction about the writing of a poem Anne and I share, although we may have come to it by separate routes. We both have very strong feelings about a poem ending definitively. We don't like poems that trail off. Real closure.

Sexton: We both do. Oscar Williams said, anyone can write a poem, but who can end it? It's like slamming the door. And I said, you mean like having sex without orgasm? He didn't like that remark.

Showalter: Do you do this exchanging with your novels as well, Maxine?

Kumin: Anne reads sections. I ask a lot from her when I write prose, but not as much these days.

Showalter: Is the poetry workshopping diminishing too? Do you do this less, need this less, than you used to?

Sexton: No, not as long as we're writing.

Kumin: I think the difference is that perhaps this year I haven't been writing as much.

Sexton: I haven't been writing as much either; I've been having an upsetting time.

Kumin: I think the intensity is the same, but the frequency has changed.

Sexton: But just the other day Maxine said, well, that's a therapeutic poem, and I said, for god's sake, forget that. I want to make it a real poem. Then I forced her into helping me make it a real poem, instead of just a kind of therapy for myself. But I remember once a long time ago a poem called "Cripples and Other Stories." I showed it to my psychoanalyst—it was half done—and I threw it in the wastebasket.

Very unusual because I usually put them away forever. But this was in the wastebasket. I said, would you by any chance be interested in what's in the wastebasket? And she said, wait a minute, Anne. You could make a real poem out of that. And you know how different that is from Maxine's voice.

Kumin: I happen to really love that poem.

Sexton: Really? I hate it. Although it's good. It reads well. But we're different temperatures, Maxine and I. I have to be warmer. We can't even be in the same room.

Kumin: I'm always taking my clothes off and Anne is putting on coats and sweaters.

Sexton: But you must remember it's not just a poetic relationship. It's been a great bond of friendship, growing, I suppose developing, deeper and deeper. I mean, if one of us is sick, the other is right there. We tell each other everything that's going on. I tell her a dream to remember it, almost. Used to—I haven't been lately. We've both been so busy this year, we've kind of drifted apart, but it's because—

Smith: When you talk about a poem, do you talk about ideas or techniques?

Kumin: Usually we don't start without a draft.

Sexton: Well—I remember you talking to me about "Eighteen Days Without You," helping me with the plot, the cabin. Although in the end I used none of it.

Kumin: You had started though. You knew the shape.

Sexton: No I didn't. I have the worksheets. First of all you had an apartment in Watertown and then I make it a cabin in Groton. Yet, she's fictionalized, helping me fictionalize the setting for the lovers. She did one thing, I did another. She started me.

Kumin: It's always been this way.

Sexton: Now can I tell this very personal thing, which we can cross out?

Kumin: Probably not, but go ahead.

Sexton: We might just be talking, and I'd say, we're just talking. Why the hell aren't we writing? And we'd get a line, a concept. I'd say, I'll call you back in twenty minutes. It is the most stimulating thing. It's a challenge. We've got this much time, and goddam it, I'm going to have something there. We hang up. In twenty-five minutes I call back. Have you got anything? She sure does. And so have I. It forces us. It's the challenge of it. And with the workshop we had, we always had two poems, sometimes three.

Kumin: There were certain people who need not be mentioned who always went over their allotted time span. My kids, when they would see some activity around the house would say, oh, the poets! now we'll *never* get any sleep! And they would fight for the privilege of sleeping over the garage, which was at the farthest remove, because the poets were so noisy. The poets came together and fought.

Sexton: We'd scream and yell. Sam Albert said to Anne Hussey: There was no one who fought harder for her words in workshop than Anne Sexton and then went home and changed them. But I would fight—it was like they were taking my babies away from me. Actually I would write down who said what— like Max, no, George, this—and there were certain people I respected more. But Sam could be good at a sort of instinctive thing.

Kumin: Well, we were a good group. George was icily cerebral. George would be sitting there counting the syllabics. But I could point to lines that I changed because of George. We've grown in different directions. We were very open and raw and new then. We were all beginners.

Sexton: I think I had my first book published then. But the one time we didn't speak about writing poems was about John. We didn't workshop, we didn't talk, we were suddenly separate.

Smith: Because your relationships with him were different?

Sexton: Yes, and I suppose our love for him was different.

Kumin: Grief is private.

Sexton: But our grief was never private in any other way. It was just with him, because he loved you, he didn't love me, and it probably made you feel guilty. Anyway, we discussed nothing. She wrote one poem, I wrote another. Mine was called "Somewhere in Africa."

Showalter: Has anything that's come out from the women's movement made you see the relationship you have in a different way?

Sexton: You see, when we began, there was no women's movement. We were it.

Kumin: And we didn't know it.

Showalter: Because the relationship you have, and the relationship of Hallie and Sukey in *The Passions of Uxport* is totally new.

Sexton: I want to say—that is not me in *The Passions of Uxport*.

Kumin: But certainly it takes something from our friendship.

Showalter: There are very few relationships in books that are like it. Women are generally supposed to destroy each other.

Sexton: I do support Maxine, although I've been a little weaker—

Kumin: Of course you do. When I was writing my first novel, Anne was in Europe on a Prix de Rome. I sent Annie air mail, what? Forty pages? Three chapters. I said, please wherever you are, drop everything, read this, get back in touch with me. I don't know what I'm doing. Am I writing a novel? And Anne read it.

Sexton: I started to cry. I was with Sandy. We had just driven out of Venice and I read the three chapters from *The Dooms of Love,* and I cried. She could do it.

Kumin: I had to do all that without her. I think though that we're always proud of ourselves that we're not dependent on the relationship. We're very autonomous people, but it *is* a nurturing relationship.

Showalter: What difference would it have made if there had been a women's movement?

Kumin: We would have felt a lot less secretive.

Sexton: Yes, we would have felt legitimate.

Kumin: We both have repressed, kept out of the public eye that we did this.

Sexton: I mean, our husbands, we could have thrown it at them.

Showalter: Why did you feel so ashamed of this mutual support?

Sexton: We did. We were ashamed. We had to keep ourselves separate.

Kumin: We were both struggling for identity.

Sexton: Also, it's a secret, we didn't want anyone to know. But I think it's time to acknowledge it.

Smith: The separateness is evident and obvious.

Sexton: You should put that in, because the people who read this might never have read us, and think we're alike. I said to Maxine, write a book called *Up Country*.

Kumin: Yes, you did. You tell yours and I'll tell mine.

Sexton: I said write those country poems. It will be a book. Have it illustrated.

Showalter: By Barbara Swan. That's one of the external things that connects you, one of the few visible signs. Barbara Swan's illustrations for *Up Country, Transformations, The Death Notebooks, Live or Die*.

Sexton: She was at the Radcliffe Institute.

Kumin: We were all there in the same year. Annie wrote the first transformation, and I said, god, that's fantastic. You could do a whole book of these. And Annie said I couldn't possibly. That's the only one, I know it. Of course, by the next day she had written another one. When she was done she said, what can I call it? And I said, call it *Transformations*.

Sexton: Right in the middle I started a novel and you said, put that novel down and finish that book of poems! And thank you.

Kumin: We titled each other's books. I titled *Transformations—*

Sexton: It's a crappy title *(laughing)*.

Kumin: I love it.

Sexton: And I named *Up Country*.

Showalter: You said you knew that could be a book. When you write do the poems come separately, or in a rush as a book?

Sexton: She had it in her to write masses of these country poems. I knew it.

Showalter: How do you organize the poems in the books?

Sexton: Well, we look at each other's things and say, do I have a book or do I not have a book? And we say, help me, help me, or this is crap.

Smith: I assume *Up Country* came thematically. In the author's note you have to *Live or Die,* you say you're going to publish the poems chronologically. Were you interested in them as biography?

Sexton: No, I just thought it might be vaguely interesting to someone to see what dates they were written. They were all dated in the manuscripts, you see.

Smith: How did they come together as a book?

Sexton: I remember George reading it, and there was no last poem. He said, all you need is a poem saying hello. And I wrote "Live."

Kumin: Funny how we both went back to George. I sent George the manuscript of my third book, and he read through it with a great deal of care.

Sexton: Some of his comments were damn wrong. He said, no one can write about operations but Anne Sexton. How ridiculous. A totally different kind of operation. I encouraged her to write it.

Showalter: There were a lot of nineteenth-century women writers who had partnerships like that, and critics tried to make them rivals. Charlotte Brontë once delayed the publication of a novel so it wouldn't come out at the same time as Elizabeth Gaskell's.

Sexton: Of course. We have books coming out at the same time next year.

Kumin: We just found out.

Sexton: It's all right. Maxine used to be horrified if we came out in the same year. But we're not compared.

Showalter: In a larger sense, now there's a female renaissance in poetry.

Kumin: Thank God. I think the fact that women are coming out of the closet is one of the most positive things that's happened in the century. Maybe the only good thing in a fucked-up world. I see such immense changes in women's perceptions. I grew up in an era when you went to a cocktail party and measured your success by how many men spoke to you. I really identified much more with the male side, but now I have such a feeling of sisterhood. I find that wherever I go, I meet splendid women, and I'd a hell of a lot rather be with them.

Sexton: You know, this is also your analysis.

Kumin: Yes, and the fact that I have two grown daughters with full-blown careers, and they have raised my consciousness. It was the work that I did with the analyst that helped me get past my awful difficulties with my own mother.

Sexton: She had no close women friends, but I broke the barrier, because I'm a terrible breaker of barriers.

Showalter: Did you have a lot of close women friends?

Sexton: Yes.

Showalter: But in your books you have generations of women—the mother, the grandmother, the daughter. There aren't any women friends in it.

Sexton: You do see Max, and lists of names. There are the dedications.

Showalter: But then there are the blood relationships that are difficult, love you have to win back.

Sexton: My mother was very destructive. The only person who was very constructive in my life was my great-aunt, and of course she went mad when I was thirteen. It was probably the trauma of my life that I never got over.

Showalter: How did she go mad?

Kumin: Read "Some Foreign Letters."

Sexton: That doesn't help. Do you know "The Hex"? "Anna Who Was Mad" in *Folly*? Notice the guilt in them. But the hex is a misnomer. I had tachycardia and I though it was just psychological.

Showalter: Were you named for her?

Sexton: Yes, we were namesakes. We had love songs we would sing together. She cuddled me. I was tall, but I tried to cuddle up. My mother never touched me in my life, except to examine me. So I had bad experiences. But I wondered with this that every summer there was Nana, and she would rub my back for hours. My mother said, women don't touch women like that. And I wondered why I didn't become a lesbian. I kissed a boy and Nana went mad. She called me a whore and everything else.

I think I'm dominating this interview.

Kumin: You are, Anne.

Showalter: Maxine, in *The Passions of Uxport* you describe the death of a child from leukemia—a death which has haunted me ever since. Do you think it's more difficult for a woman to write about the death of a child?

Kumin: In all my novels there's a death. In *The Abduction* there's a sixteen-year-old who dies in a terrible car crash. Perhaps as a mother I have a fear of a loss of a child.

Sexton: We all know that a child going is the worst suffering.

Kumin: Many years ago, my brother lost a child, and I remember this terrible Spartan funeral. That's the funeral in *The Passions of Uxport,* when he says the Hebrew prayer for the dead.

Sexton: Do you remember we were young and going to a place called the New England Poetry Club, the first year we won the prizes, first or second. We were terrified. It was our first reading. Maxine's voice was trembling so, we couldn't hear her.

Kumin: I couldn't breathe.

Sexton: I couldn't stand up, I was shaking so. I sat on the table.

Kumin: I wonder if there was a trembling in us—the wicked mother, or the wicked witch, or whatever those ladies were to us.

Showalter: They were all women?

Kumin: There were a few squashy old men.

Sexton: There were young men too. John was there. Sam was there.

Showalter: Did you have trouble with women writers of another generation? In Louise Bogan's *Letters*—she says about Anne? She doesn't seem to have been able to accept the subjects.

Kumin: This was the problem with a great many people. Women are not supposed to have uteruses, especially in poems.

Sexton: To me, there's nothing that can't be talked about in art. But I hate the way I'm anthologized in women's lib anthologies. They cull out the "hate men" poems, and leave nothing else. They show only one little aspect of me. Naturally there are times I hate men, who wouldn't? But there are times I love them. The feminists are doing themselves a disservice to show just this.

Kumin: They'll get over that.

Sexton: Yes, but by then, they won't be published. Therefore they've lost their chance.

Showalter: When I anthologized you in my book, *Women's Liberation and Literature,* I chose "Abortion," "Housewife," and "For My Lover on Returning to His Wife." And I like all those poems very much; I'd choose them again.

Sexton: "For My Lover" is a help. It doesn't cost very much money to get "Housewife"—you can get it cheap. A strange thing—"a woman *is* her mother." That's how it ends. A housecleaner—washing herself down, washing the house. It was about my mother-in-law.

Showalter: A woman is her mother-in-law.

With Gregory Fitz Gerald

At the time of her suicide on Friday, October 4, 1974, Anne Sexton had achieved widespread fame as a poet. Winner of the Pulitzer Prize for Poetry in 1967 (for Live or Die*), her books include* To Bedlam and Part Way Back *(1960),* All My Pretty Ones *(1962),* Love Poems *(1969),* Transformations *(1971),* The Book of Folly *(1972),* The Death Notebooks *(1974), and the posthumous* The Awful Rowing Toward God *(1975). The interview was taped at Anne Sexton's home in Weston, Massachusetts, on June 24, 1974. [G. F.]*

To what extent do poetic traditions affect you? Any tradition: English, American, European, or even Asiatic?

Spanish; of course, it's all through translation: Pablo Neruda . . . I suppose the Surrealists: Rimbaud, Baudelaire . . . But I'm what they call a "primitive," because I don't know much.

Then it's an intelligent ignorance; Democritus long ago pointed out that "we know nothing, for truth lies in the depth."

Reprinted with permission from the *Massachusetts Review* 19 (1978), Copyright © 1978 The Massachusetts Review, Inc. Also with permission from A. Gregory Fitz Gerald, editor and interviewer.

Yes; anyway, my influences are very, very limited because I haven't had time to read enough. I did not go to college; I was not taught anything.

I was all alone. My major influence was W. D. Snodgrass, before his first book [*Heart's Needle*, 1959] was published, only because he was doing, it seemed to me, what I was starting to do, or trying to do, couldn't help doing.

I was writing personal poetry, often about the subject of madness. Everyone said, "You can't write that way!" Then suddenly I read "Heart's Needle," and I think, "Dear God, I am moved!"

The contrasting literary atmosphere then was a highly academic one; some would say "boring"?

All I know is that most poetry I was reading then was boring *me*. I might admire some. Poets weren't exciting me, weren't moving me. Not that I thought *I* was very good, or anything like that, but I thought, he doesn't have to be boring.

Are you saying that some of the early postwar poetry was overintellectualized, overliterary?

Yes. Blah, blah, blah. I really couldn't get too excited. But when I read about the loss of a child in "Heart's Needle," the lyricism, the beauty, and the feeling of a father, I immediately identify, and zoom, that moves me into action. There is a poem! But my own daughter [Joy] was not a needle in my heart. It was the *loss* of her; *that* was the needle in my heart. At that time she wasn't living with me; I had a nervous breakdown. And Snodgrass's poem moved me to get her back. But I wasn't ready to keep her at that point. God! Here is a poem making me wash up, get in my car, grab my child, and say, "She's mine; I'm taking her home!" But this was Joy, a baby, and it just didn't work out. There were too many things working against it. Joy left home at nine months and stayed away for a year and a half. I can't remember. I can just say my own poem ["The Double Image" in *To Bedlam and Part Way Back*] was provided by the loss of a child, but in a fictionalized way. I'd actually met someone in a mental hospital who'd had an illegitimate child. So I understood the loss of a child. It wouldn't help to say that I have another daughter [Linda]; she's right here, because you have to change a little bit for . . .

. . . for the fictionalized purposes of art?

Yes, eliminating some facts is not so much the point. It would distract from the image of the loss.

You're talking about the artistic necessity of concentrated effect?

I didn't understand that; I just did it.

Instinctively; and that implies that for you instinct is a more important attribute than . . .

I can say it ["The Double Image"] is written in very strict form, and that I didn't know much. I made up my own form. I worked very hard from section to section, it being a long poem, to have a different pace. I didn't think of it when I was writing it, but in retrospect I guess I was trying to give it a symphonic quality. Something in me said, jeepers, you're not going to go on forever! Now let's do *this*. I'm pushing for the reality, the truth, and yet I'm trying to change it a little—not just the rhythm—not anything that easy.

From the back of your psyche are you making some kind of statement?

No; I just wanted to write the poem as well as possible. I never thought about my readers too much.

You just said, "symphonic," reminding me that you use music as a background for your writing.

Music creates a certain mood in me. I might write for six months to one side of one record. Then I might suddenly switch and say "no," but it would just be a funny feeling. I'd feel around in my record collection for what's right. It can never have words, unless they're foreign words, because that's not distracting.

You like the human voice?

I love the human voice, and I love the lyrics. Yet, I can't listen to words if I'm writing words; but in a language I don't know, it doesn't matter. Words become another instrument, or a kind of choir from the soul. The Laurindo Almedia/Sally Terri record—especially the Villa Lobos song,[1] moves me very deeply. I don't think there's any influence, exactly, unless it's so unconscious that I'm absolutely unaware of it. I'm not even following the rhythm.

Is yours a conscious approach to poetic rhythm or is it quite natural?

Natural, unless I want to use syllabic beat. But that's what I call "tricks."

What's an example of your "tricks"?

"The Double Image," probably "The Division of Parts" [in *To Bedlam and Part Way Back*], and "Eighteen Days Without You" [in *Love Poems*]. And I cheat, or if I haven't cheated, I'll cheat later, so no one can see this dreadful dreck I'm doing.

What kind of cheating is that?

Add a syllable. But I don't make them up as some arbitrary thing. I write the first stanza; here it is. Then I count out the syllables. I make it look like I feel it. If I want to, I can suddenly break it and go into something else. It's mere dreckery to get the poem out, which is the important thing. At first I don't plan anything out. But once it's there, then I figure it all out. If you start going down the page, it's very easy to see me cheating, writing eight or nine or four.

And some examples of the natural?

I really don't know. When people say the rhythm is off, I can't do much about it, because my rhythms are very unconscious, a kind of natural flow. I might say, "This poem is one long sentence, run on." But you can't read it all in one breath! I want it to be like a snapshot, to have the quality of a candid photograph.

Your interview with Patricia Marx . . .

That was first a radio interview and Patricia Marx published it.*

. . . you said that poets are always fighting to find out what it is they want to say, implying that poets often don't know in advance, implying that writing the poem is itself a process of psychological, intellectual, and emotional discovery.

Yes, that often can happen. An image might come to me, a line—you don't know where it's going to go. It goes its own way.

Isn't the writing of poetry a process of discovery?

Most often, I guess. It's very hard to be that conscious of what you're doing.

Even when reading it over afterwards?

If I really did know I might not have been able to write it! I certainly don't study my poems and ask, "What exactly is going on here?" I might not be so good at writing the next one; I might not be able to go that deep.

You'd prefer not to delve too deeply into what's going on?

---

*Reprinted in this volume, pp. 70–82.—ED.

Absolutely! Or else I might not be able to do it again, because something might block me and say, "Hey, wait a minute, I'm not sure I want to know that" (the superego or ego or whatever). I'm not saying I don't read them and couldn't explicate them.

But you'd rather not?

Sometimes I do. There's always discovery; but how deep it goes depends on each poem.

What about the difference between your interpretation of your own poem and that of some famous critic?

I think it'd be interesting.

Do you think either one or the other would be valid, or do you think both interpretations might be valid?

To both my daughters I've said, "Look, if you like the poem, don't let anyone tell you what it means. Because it means what *you* think it means." And they got in horrible trouble.

That seems to deny objective reality in poetry.

Wait a minute. It takes it away from the reader to say, "It means *this*." It ceases, then, to belong to that reader.

You're asking your readers to have a personal experience?

Yes, and let them have it! Don't rob them of it—too early, anyway. Later on—way, way later on—let someone tell them what it means, give opinions, including the writer's, who might not know either.

You said earlier you're not too willing to explicate a poem's meaning.

You might be fooling yourself or lying to yourself. The critic might be way off, too. If you look into enough criticism, that can be well established. That's factual.

Yes.

But the poem should be what it means to its *readers*. They can grow with it. If some reader really likes a poem, he might read it five years later and see in it something very different, because he's lived a little longer and suddenly sees something very startlingly new. But if he were informed of it then, he might not be ready, or it may not be wanted or needed. I'm not talking about poems that are stuffed down your throat. I feel that the poems I love by other people belong to *me*. I don't need to hear what these poems mean, because they may have a meaning so deep I don't *want* to know.

Does that have anything to do with your attempts to rewrite earlier published poems?

Let me begin this way. I started rewriting the first poem ["You, Doctor Martin"] in the first book [*To Bedlam and Part Way Back*] because I would never write it now with those dreadful inversions! Someone said, "But you're ruining it." I said, "But it's not right." And then someone said, "But you're taking something away." And I said, "But I know the good lines in this poem, and I can see such terrible flaws!" Then I thought: Let it stand. Let the whole damned thing stand, for better or worse. Don't go back and rewrite, trying to make a masterpiece out of everything. Leave it alone.

If I went back and rewrote those early poems, they'd all take on the same voice now present. It's always the same words. But it does change somewhat, it does evolve, it does do different things, thematically. Say you took the poem and just wanted to make it a better poem. What's all this business about going back and rewriting and rewriting, making it better and better, after it's in book form? I don't mean to say that if you printed a poem in a magazine—because then you still rewrite. Once it's in book form, the public has it; it's in the anthologies. Then you go switching it all around. I call this goddamned confusing. I want what was there. Talk about spontaneity! At least *that* much. I don't want a poem constantly revised, every minute. Many writers do it, and I don't criticize them. But I think, look, Anne, is this the best thing to do, or wouldn't you rather go on and write a new poem? Maybe the new poems are not as good as the early ones, but wouldn't you rather go on? If you want to say something, say it *again*, with new insight. Don't go back and pull this poem up and do surgery on it! You're a different human being. I do think, in a kind of blind, foolish irrational way: the new poem might be good enough, to document in some form or other, however vaguely, the observations, inner or outer—mostly inner—of one life, however brief its span may be. I see everyone as writing the same poem, only with many voices. We're all writing the poem of our time, everyone differently. So *my* name is Anne Sexton, who lives here in Massachusetts out in Weston, the suburbs of Boston. I'm just one woman, who was a child, who is going through life, whatever life might bring forth.

It happens I love to read journals, biographies (but I prefer *autobiography,* though I think then one has to lie more than otherwise). When I touch another life, from any era, I'm fascinated. Then I know more than if I read history. This is just me; it's a kind of hang-up. It might also be my rationale for writing what they call "professional poetry" (sic).

You said, "This is just me." Isn't the me *natural?*

I hope so, or else there's absolutely no point to it. There's something universal in one person: death, the cold facts, and all that. These aren't quite as important as how you master them, your reaction, or the imagery, or the way it's brought forth, or the story it tells. If you sat down and said, "This is my life." Like to a psychoanalyst, you might say, "Okay, we've got an hour; I'll tell you my history." Snap, snap, snap. You couldn't really do it in one hour, of course. But if you'd written it all out beforehand, in just a minimal outline, "Here are the horrors of my life; here are the good things of my life." It would be rather dull: it wouldn't have any substance. . . .

You can see that I don't think so rationally. A friend of mine said my interviews are terrible. He said, "You don't listen to the question, dope! You give some vague reply." Sometimes the question doesn't *mean* anything to me. I can't absorb it. It just goes right over me.

You can answer whatever question you want to, as far as I'm concerned.

I go off, way off. I just wander. But go ahead.

Is it true that your frame of reference is ultimately religious? That's what A. R. Jones stated about your poetry nearly ten years ago.[2]

I'd love to reread it. It was a long time ago, when he wrote that. I call that kind of a prophecy of what was . . .

. . . what was to be in later books?

The Death Notebooks is certainly religious, I guess. But I don't know what "religious" means, really.

I find religion in The Death Notebooks *and in your new book called* The Awful Rowing Toward God . . .

. . . which is coming out in early 1975. It might be that Jones found my poems religious, in a broad sense, without their being overtly religious at all.

It's puzzling, it's interesting, to see what someone would perceive; you think, isn't that fascinating! It could be the child's delight, as in building a sand castle and then having a king walk out of it! That's hyperbole, of course, but the child's delight is saying, "What! I did that? I didn't know I was doing that!" Then you have this amazed feeling, perhaps I'm really doing *that!* I didn't know it at all. You have this sense of sharp surprise.

One can't help feeling that The Awful Rowing Toward God *is a kind of spiritual quest. That's why I find it an end point for which one could, in retrospect, discover beginnings in the earlier work, in* Transformations, *and even much earlier in* To Bedlam and Part Way Back.

What you have in mind is the interview* where the interviewer keeps asking about my religious poems. I keep saying, "I don't want to talk about them." And I wouldn't. Yet, she kept right on asking, after all that.

Do you still feel that way?

No, now it's all right; but I was unconsciously resisting then. I can surmise now that it was there all along, but I wasn't ready; if I talked about it, it might . . .

. . . might hurt it in some way?

. . . because I wasn't conscious of it, and I wasn't going to admit to it, until it swept me up. Actually [*The Awful Rowing Toward God*] was written like I've written nothing else: in two and a half weeks.

In two and a half weeks?

With three days out. One for exhaustion and two for a mental hospital. Then out and back to the book. Staying up till three A.M., and getting up again at six. Writing in seizure, practically not stopping; maybe not even drinking; maybe just gobbling my meal and running back in there and writing again. The poems were coming too fast to rewrite.

---

*With Barbara Kevles, reprinted in this volume, pp. 83–111.—Ed.

Almost a compulsion?

Not a "compulsion." I hate to use the word because there must be a better one. But could I say "a seizure of inspiration"? Compulsion puts it on the level of neurosis, although certainly there are plenty of analysts who would say that belief in God is irrational and irrelevant. And I did speak with a priest.

Father Dunn?

Yes, Father Dunn. This was when I was in a mental hospital. I only met him once or twice, but I knew he was very familiar with my poetry. He just came and sat down, and I said, "Well, I've lost it all."

I'm sure you're quite aware that this search for God, the spiritual, is really quite different from the tendency of our time. Many other poets seem to have lost, not found, God.

I don't even know. I said to Father Dunn, "Look, I'm not sure I believe in God, anyway." And he was sitting there just reading my poems to me, and he said, "Your typewriter is your altar." I said, "I can't go to church. I can't pray." He said, "Your poems are your prayers." He was not a particularly intellectual person, but he was wise enough merely to read my poems back to me, to fill me with hope. As he left me, he said, "Get out of here; you don't belong in here. Come on back to the typewriter!" And I said, "Pray for me." He said, "No, you pray for me."

It just happened; that's all I can tell you. It was a marvel. Remember, there's no Catholicism in my family, really, except on my father's side.

It does seem a movement toward Catholicism.

Why should it be? I've called it: him, she, God. I call it, "my funny God."

In The Awful Rowing Toward God *you write about the crucifix-ion, about Mary, the mother of God, using numerous religious images that specifically suggest a Roman Catholic orientation.*

But don't forget Who's Jewish!

No, of course not. But in a time when religion is so unfashionable!

I can't help that. I write what I must. I can't worry about fashion and never could—from the very beginning, when they said, "You can't write that way," to this very moment.

You don't find something very *fashionable, such as Zen Buddhism; you go back toward Christianity.*

I'm not so sure it's always Christianity.

Yet you write about Jesus Christ, you talk about crucifixion, you talk about Mary . . .

Not every minute.

No, not every minute, but I'm not inventing all this!

Yes. I know that.

I'm talking about The Awful Rowing Toward God, *something I've just finished reading.*

All right, what was the last poem? Is that the Christian God? Is that the Roman Catholic God?

That's not impossible.

It's very strange that God sits on the rocks of the island you've been rowing to . . .

. . . dealing poker . . .

. . . playing a poker hand we're dealt.

May I quote you, please?

Yes.

"Dearest dealer, / I with my royal straight flush, / love you so for your wild card, / that untamable, eternal, gut-driven ha-ha */ and lucky love." End of "The Rowing Endeth" and of the book.*

But here he is laughing: he is slumped over me laughing, and I'm laughing. He didn't beat me; we both won!

But he had a wild card and came up with five aces!

Five aces, because I had a royal straight flush, and I think I won, but I didn't hear him announce the wild card, 'cause I'm in such awe sitting on the rocks there on the island with God, playing a poker game. Would that fit into your religious construction?

It not only can . . .

I don't see why *anything* can't. Do you think the Pope would say Okay?

I'm not a theologian.

A good pope would.

Would Father Dunn?

Oh yes, Father Dunn would. But I said to Father Dunn, "I wish you would come in here and baptize me, and I'd take communion." He said, "You've got to do the studies," and all that stuff. I said, "Look, I can't do that, Father Dunn, because it would ruin, it would formulate, my thinking: I'd want him to be *my* God, anyway. I don't want to be taught about him; I want to make him up."

Your poetry in The Awful Rowing Toward God *is in fine company: George Herbert, John Donne, John Milton . . .*

. . . you mean in subject matter?

Yes. St. John of the Cross, and others too numerous to mention. Did I misunderstand you earlier? Weren't you objecting a little to my suggestion that you were involved in a tradition?

In an orthodox traditional religion, yes. Because I don't know about it.

But, at least, in the sense that you're using poetry for spiritual discovery.

Of course, *that* tradition. But talking about tradition in a particular denomination . . .

I'm being more general than that.

That's why I'm fighting the Roman Catholic attribution, although I did talk to a priest. I would hope very much that a Jew would like this poem.

Nondenominationalism?

That's exactly what I mean; except that, I don't know as orientals would . . .

But the fact that John Donne was an Anglican doesn't bother other Protestant readers, or Roman Catholics, or Jews—I mean in experiencing the spiritual impact.

No, but I didn't want to categorize, that's all. I don't want it to come out of tradition or to be learned, because I just don't *know* that much.

Here you are, Anne Sexton, 1974, and you do belong to another tradition, a Yankee, New England tradition that goes back to the governors of Maine and even farther . . .

My great-grandfather [Nelson Dingley, 1832–99, governor of Maine 1874–76; U.S. House of Representatives 1888–99] attended church, understand, but also traveled on the Continent a long time ago, probably around 1860. He traveled in Europe, and I don't know if he was governor at the time—he was an editor of a newspaper [*Lewiston Evening Journal*] anyway. He had twelve children, and he decorated his home with a great interest in the arts. He had a strong personality, and the minister/preacher came to his home and said, "You can't come to church if you keep these nude statues in your house!" He said, "In that case I will not go to church." He sat his twelve children in a circle around him every Sunday morning, and for two hours they could not move as he read the Bible.

That minister showed a narrowness . . .

Yes! I like my grandfather, although, thank God, I wasn't one of his children sitting there for two hours; but maybe he was interesting.

He saw nothing wrong with the body's beauty.

I call that religious. He was his own man. I can say, yes, there is his tradition, a Yankee tradition. I know this because my uncle did a genealogy, and it goes back to kings and queens, who intermarry all over Europe. It was of interest to me. An interested niece found him living in Florida, a retired Navy Admiral. He made genealogy a great hobby, had looked up the whole thing. It was interesting to see the intermarriage, and where it would go. It's funny; they were supposed to be the scum, those who came over here on the *Mayflower*.

The relationship . . . ?

It was actually William Brewster, I don't know much about him; so I never get to know.

If you could time-travel back to their era, and have them read your poetry, they would probably be shocked.

Shocked! I'd probably be *executed,* put in an iron maiden. The Puritans would have burned me at the stake, of course.

Samuel Sewall would have regarded your poetry as witchcraft. The Puritans would have said you're a sensual woman, concerned with the human body, its potentialities.

I'm very concerned with relationships, with human beings, love; just the touch of two fingers is immediate contact. Holding the hand can go as far as sexual intercourse, like in *Love Poems.* I open the book with "The Touch," "The Kiss," "The Breast," and it goes on physically. Of course, it's from a woman's standpoint, though not always. "The Touch" shows something about my feeling that there's God everywhere, although I didn't know it when I was writing it. It all begins how there's no touch ("For months my hand had been sealed off / in a tin box.") The last stanza goes: "Then all this became history." "All this" is the loss, the abandoned hand:

> Then all this became history.
> Your hand found mine.
> Life rushed to my fingers like a blood clot.
> Oh, my carpenter,
> the fingers are rebuilt.
> They dance with yours.
> They dance in the attic and in Vienna.
> My hand is alive all over America.
> Not even death will stop it,
> death shedding her blood.
> Nothing will stop it, for this is the kingdom
> and the kingdom come.

I just wrote that. I didn't look into it. But now in retrospect, I think, "This is the kingdom / and the kingdom come." I must have seen God and the kingdom, the eternal.

But how does that relate to sensuality, to physicalness?

I am saying in *that* is God. To take it a step further, in *The Death Notebooks* there's a series of poems called "The Furies." One is called "The Fury of Cocks."

You don't mean roosters.

No, I mean cocks:

> She is the house.
> He is the steeple.
> When they fuck they are God.
> When they break away they are God.
> When they snore they are God.
> In the morning they butter the toast.
> They don't say much.
> They are still God.
> All the cocks of the world are God,
> blooming, blooming, blooming
> into the sweet blood of woman.

Now I become much more directly sexual, instead of just touch. I'm saying, "When they fuck they are God . . . [and] When they snore. . . ."

Your God image is a regenerative one, as indeed sexual intercourse can become the making of a human being . . .

We have the Pill and all that. We're not always making another human being. We always *wish* we were, kind of; it's natural.

Though we may wish unconsciously . . .

Yes. Consciously, we wish we *aren't;* but there is this unconsciousness . . .

That ambivalence.

There are certainly people who don't want children, ever.

That's what some women's liberationists say.

It's hard to bring up children.

It's a full-time job.

It's even harder. Maybe mothers want to do something else, to create a statue. But whatever they want to do, maybe the bringing up of children would so interrupt, they couldn't do it. Other writers have said, "Oh no, I have to give up." I started writing while my children were awfully young. I just simply wrote when they went to sleep until three in the morning, and then got up at six. I don't know how I did it then, because now I need all my sleep. I had to; I had no choice. As they got a little older and were running around more, playing, I'd turn on a symphony, just to cut down on their noise. They would come in and break right into a poem. You get used to that; you adjust to it. "She hit me. She pinched me." Or there's always the Band-aid. We've got to get out the Band-aid, *quick.* "I fell down. Kiss it, and make it well." Or, "I want a cookie." Millions of things go wrong. They might be out lighting matches, burning up leaves. You've got to be *aware.* It's difficult, but not impossible. There was no women's lib when I was starting. As a matter of fact, it was very shocking that I wrote so personally about a woman. I wrote a certain poem called "Menstruation at Forty" [in *Live or Die*], and a very fine critic made some very disparaging remark that was such a good put-down to the poem! But if we'd had women's lib, there would have been an awful lot of letters coming in to *Harper's* magazine. That remark, "Really, what is this talk of menstruation? You don't *use* words like that." It amuses me now because I'm forty-five, and I wrote it when I was thirty-five and I thought "Menstruation at Forty," that'll be a nice opening. I feel younger now at forty-five than I did at thirty-five. But we were talking about the body. If you look at that poem, there's an awful lot about the children she wants, the loss. The son . . .

The son?

Yes, it's the only poem I ever really wrote about wanting a son, I think. I say, "Susan, David, David, David," just being two favorite names.

An unfulfilled craving?

No, no, just . . . a very small part of something I was writing about right then. For a woman not to have a son is, is . . . I used to say, "Dear God, it's good I didn't have a son, because I don't quite understand men very well."

No one believes that you "don't understand men very well."

I see men as human beings. Like women's lib, I believe in men's lib. We'd soon better come to men's lib. Because many men are stuck in dreadful jobs they loathe: from working in an automobile factory, a plastics factory, or a coal mine to a simple office job, to a stockbroker, or to whatever. He would love to throw it all over, but he's got to bring home the bread for the wife, who is very unhappy bringing up these draggy kids. She sweats all day. And it *was* a horrible day! If everyone could be liberated, could be fulfilled, it would be wonderful, marvelous. It's too bad that women couldn't rise up and free the men somehow. If they could be paid well enough, they could say, "Wait a minute. Let *me* go to work. You stay at home." Maybe you want to become a photographer, or whatever. This is very hypothetical, one little drama in the perhaps world of never-never land. But then you might say, "There ought to be children's lib!" Then you think, Well, not *too* much. There's been a little bit too much children's lib here. There should be a slight turn every generation. But this younger generation are a real switch. I think they're experimenting with sex too soon for their psychological health and growth. For a female it's a much more important commitment. (That's probably a sexist remark.) I've seen it happen to young women. Lately drugs are starting to drop off, and that's good because there's no point in going out of your mind on purpose. That seems to be a bit unnecessary. [. . .]

An inability to believe in anything seems one of the characteristics of our age. If one can believe in the body, in God, in sex, and in life, then that's positive.

And in the grass growing and in wood walls not yet scooped up by a tornado . . .

. . . and women free from the bonds the past shackled them with.

It's terrible, when you think way back—the male names . . .

George Eliot, and others.

And then let's think of the current sexual freedom, now that gay lib is okay. Nobody gets too upset. People say, "Well, so what?" That's what the younger generation has given to us. "Be what you are!" We can learn from that.

We should and can learn from the young?

Yes. We can learn from them, and we can teach them, just vaguely. Certainly no one learns much from *your* experience. They can learn from theirs. But—this kind of freedom started with the young; it started with the women's movement. It probably goes back to Dr. Spock. We ought to elect him king. Every kid was a little brought up on Dr. Spock. Mothers running in and looking up the disease. "What is this, measles? What do I do?" There was a certain freedom; it was one of the larger influences in bringing up children in this country. It's damned good.

He released you from some of the earlier inhibitions?

No, except if I got a little bit scared, I'd run in and look it up. You can say "inhibitions" in society, but I'm talking about the multiple individuals making up society. There are different mores and strictures within all segments of society. So how can one merely generalize? To a large degree maybe it's just the middle class that was so influenced by Spock. It's strange; it's as though, "Dear me, here's this baby!" I thought, I don't know how to do this. I've had no younger brothers or sisters. I had this psychiatrist, who said, "Please throw out every book on child care. You can keep the Spock, because you can look up the diseases. Follow your instinct. You're a mother; it's okay."

That fits your notion of poetry, to follow your instincts. Sometimes it's damned good.

Sometimes it's damned bad. But that's not usually your instinct. It's something getting in the way, I think, probably magic, the unconscious, and the depths; what I would say calling forth the muse. Evoke her, as she drops down in a little string bag from God; or, as you pull her forth, fork her, and tear her out of your unconscious. Or she just happens to float by like a little butterfly, like a "given poem," as we would say. "This poem just came, that's all: I did nothing to get it."

Have the net unfurled, ready as the butterfly wings by.

It's what we call a gift from the muse. It happens so seldom. And it might not have more than one word to correct.

It might come during the night?

Never with me, no. But to some, of course.

Coming back to women's lib, how do you think that's affecting contemporary poetry?

There are many more women writing, writing like mad, expressing themselves.

Women form a much larger proportion of the total number of writers today.

You see writing classes with many more women than men. I would surmise that in the early 1950s, there were predominantly men. Women didn't think they could be poets.

If they did, perhaps they were preoccupied with other problems, other notions, and they may have repressed the desire.

But why, why? Women *are* creative! It was hard to get into the workshops.

No, I don't think it was so extremely hard. We have some marvelous examples from the 1950s, but they certainly were outnumbered by men. Wasn't it because of the way the culture was going?

They didn't have enough belief in themselves to attempt it.

Yes, and society was pushing them toward marriage. That was set up as an establishment ideal.

Go and get married, have babies, and be happy. That's the Hollywood dream. In our generation, we grew up with the movies, and at a certain age . . .

. . . you married and lived happily ever after.

It goes right back to the fairy tales.

Today we are very much aware that the moment marriage takes place, it's anything but happily ever after. That's where all the problems begin, not end.

That's a dismal outlook.

It may be dismal, but it seems to be true.

I happen to be newly divorced, but I didn't feel that way about it. I can't say that every moment was happy. And I can't say marriage and children were the answer for me.

Then aren't you proving my point?

Not at all, because I'm disagreeing violently that that's when the problems begin.

You thought you had bigger problems before you got married?

There were more problems, but they were other things. Dating can get boring in itself.

So can marriage.

I suppose. I didn't get divorced because I was bored. I understand marriage can get boring. I know a lot of people who are bored with their marriage.

You say, "That's when the problems begin." There are adjustments to make, certainly. I remember hearing years ago people saying, "The worst year of marriage was the first one. That was such a period of adjustment."

Isn't there a constant adjustment?

It didn't seem so to me. It was an utter delight to have someone to live with and share, and the adjustment itself was a delight.

And preoccupying, no doubt.

Preoccupying? No. I had a pal; I had my freedom; I had, oh, you could name so many things. I had the father that never loved me, loving me. I didn't have children (it was a while before we had children, because we eloped at nineteen). We were children together, playing house. What else could you say?

Many marriages begin that early or earlier.

I wouldn't suggest it, because you change too much. Here I went and had this terrible change at twenty-seven, had a nervous breakdown and all that jazz he hadn't really planned on.

You became a writer at twenty-seven and not before?

I started to write then; let's put it that way. I did write in high school for about six months, but my mother said I plagiarized; so I stopped writing, my mother being the final say.

Whom were you plagiarizing?

Sara Teasdale; that's about all I knew. Besides I wasn't *plagiarizing* her. I just sounded like her.

But now with your experience as a teacher, you know that many young people do begin with a conscious imitation of someone they love, respect, and admire.

Perhaps, but I don't see that too much in my classes. I think they're a little bit beyond that. They'll have favorite poets but they're trying to find their own voices.

Everyone'll say, "Oh, we can see so and so in her [Anne Sexton's] work." Blah, blah, blah. A lot of those things I hadn't even read! I should have, of course, but having not gone to college, having not really existed in any school whatsoever, but just as a body sitting in a chair.

Sometimes it doesn't matter whether you read something or not; it's in the air.

I did read nonfiction and fiction; so many different things will stimulate me, not just poetry.

Earlier, you talked about the apprentice-master relationship in writing as a good thing.

I think it would be the perfect way to learn.

That occurred much earlier, historically, in the teaching of writing. Masters put their students to work deliberately imitating the work of others. The fear of many contemporary students has been whether or not they would lose their own individuality, their own style, and be too imitative.

Just reading other writers?

No, by consciously imitating the forms and structures of other artists.

I might agree with *structures,* in order to learn technique—"tricks," as I call it. Somebody had student writers just sit down and retype someone else's work.

Getting it by osmosis.

It would be an interesting way.

I've heard claims that it works.

I've never tried it.

Apparently the individual doing it develops in such a way that the imitativeness eventually passes . . .

If it doesn't, then you're . . .

. . . finished, merely a bad copy. But it does seem to pass.

You should see my early work! It's so horrible. I scream at the thought of it. I have "destroy" written all over it. You would agree in a minute. It's like some baby writing.

That makes you more understanding and sympathetic with others going through similar pains?

I've never taught anyone who was as bad as I was at twenty-eight.

You mean that quite seriously?

Yes, I'm quite serious. I was—way, way in the beginning. You know the old saying? It's so much genius, so much . . . ?

Ninety percent perspiration and ten percent inspiration.

"Sweat." Or "stubbornness." I don't care if it doesn't rhyme; I want it to be accurate. Stubbornness is one of the most important qualities you could have. I will not let this get me down. I will learn it. I will master it.

And the ability to experience the killer kind of teacher without bad effects.

Yes, that's where the stubbornness comes in. I say to my class sometimes, "I think I ought to import a real bastard; so you would be ready for the life of a writer." Teaching should be nurturing, though critical. If you had a constant bastard beating you down, it might be hard. You've got to go forward. And almost everything can go wrong: rejection slips, book publishers turning you down, everything. My students may not be poets; some turn into prose writers, some turn into playwrights, even though they're in a poetry class. I have these little medals I give to people: "Don't let the bastards get you." I ought to give one as a present to every single student who graduates from my class. I try to tell them, "You think you're going to get a teaching job? Prepare to be milkmen or busmen or to drive cabs. You've got a hard climb, particularly in poetry. As a novelist you might hit it and make a lot of money."

Even if you make it into the higher echelons as a poet, it still isn't going to make you much money. Except, perhaps, from poetry readings.

That's where the real money is.

To what extent do you think poetry readings affect the poem itself? If you know in advance you're going to read a poem aloud, does that change anything?

My God, who knows in advance that you are going to read a poem? . . . I can learn an awful lot about a poem in the rewriting stage. Anybody can read it to me, whether or not they're a good reader, just so I can *hear* it. Because when *I* look at it, I can't see it objectively enough. The more unpracticed the voice, the more objective I can get. It's like becoming my own teacher. I just discovered it about a month ago.

Notes

1. "Bachianas Brasileiras No. 5," side one, band two, *Duets with the Spanish Guitar,* Angel S–36050.
2. A. R. Jones, "Necessity and Freedom: The Poetry of Robert Lowell, Sylvia Plath and Anne Sexton," *Critical Quarterly* 7 (1965):25.

UNDER DISCUSSION
David Lehman, General Editor
Donald Hall, Founding Editor

Volumes in the Under Discussion series collect reviews and essays about
individual poets. The series is concerned with contemporary American and
English poets about whom the consensus has not yet been formed and the
final vote has not been taken. Titles in the series include: